25
INVESTMENT
CLASSICS

25
INVESTMENT
CLASSICS

....

*Insights from
the Greatest
Investment Books
of all Time*

LEO GOUGH

FINANCIAL TIMES
PITMAN PUBLISHING

MANAGEMENT

LONDON · SAN FRANCISCO
KUALA LUMPUR · JOHANNESBURG

*Financial Times Management delivers the knowledge,
skills and understanding that enable students,
managers and organisations to achieve their ambitions,
whatever their needs, wherever they are*

London Office:
128 Long Acre, London WC2E 9AN
Tel: +44 (0)171 447 2000
Fax: +44 (0)171 240 5771
Website: www.ftmanagement.com

A Division of Financial Times Professional Limited

First published in Great Britain 1998

ISBN 0 273 63244 2

British Library Cataloguing in Publication Data
A CIP catalogue record for this book can be obtained
from the British Library.

10 9 8 7 6 5 4 3 2

Typeset by Northern Phototypesetting Co. Ltd, Bolton
Printed and bound in Great Britain by Biddles Ltd, Guildford & King's Lynn

*The Publishers' policy is to use paper manufactured
from sustainable forests.*

ABOUT THE AUTHOR

Leo Gough is a financial journalist and a dedicated private investor. He is the author of several books, including: *The Financial Times Guide to Business Numeracy*, *How the Stock Market Really Works*, *Going Offshore* (Financial Times Pitman Publishing) and *Asia Meltdown* (Capstone). He is also the UK editor of *Taipan*, a newsletter on direct equity investment in emerging markets.

To David Murphy,
a great humorist and
a true friend

CONTENTS

CONTENTS

INTRODUCTION

This book is a companion guide to 25 classics from the spectrum of investment writing, many of them that generations of investors have bought and read, in some cases again and again. They solve the basic problem of the private investor, which is – where do you go to learn? You can't always trust the professionals, and the markets can be an expensive place to acquire your investing wisdom without any guidance.

Good investment books are your answer. They can introduce you to new ideas, warn you off common pitfalls, allow you to learn from the mistakes of others and help you to develop your own path to that elusive beast, investment wisdom. They're cheaper than seminars or correspondence courses, and certainly cheaper than learning by blindly doing. They also help you to refine that intangible sense of judgement that you can't gain from newspapers, magazines and newsletters and that ultimately only experience can teach.

Many new investors, however, are put off by the prospect of having to read a pile of volumes before purchasing their first stock. This is the reason that I wrote this book: to provide, in one place, an introduction and critique of 25 of the most important investment books for investors, new and experienced, who haven't yet gotten around to reading them all. It is not intended to be a substitute for the classics, which, I believe, all investors should eventually read for themselves. Rereading many of them, I was reassured of the value of returning to these books again and again. There's always something new to learn, or some different perspective to help you hone your own personal investment methods.

"The most important thing in life isn't money, it's love," goes an old joke, "but I'm lucky. I love money." You might think that this was the philosophy of the authors of the 25 investment classics discussed in this book, but it isn't so. What most of them really love, it would seem, is the process, the art, of making money in the financial markets. "Money," many of them seem to say, "is only the way you keep your score in the game."

This is not to suggest that great investors aren't motivated to get rich. The majority of them started life at a disadvantage. They were born into poor families, like Benjamin Graham, were the children of refugees, like George Soros, or suffered major setbacks such as the death of their fathers at a young age, like Peter Lynch. While you can substantially increase your wealth in the markets as a passive investor, the really big money is made by a few successful professionals who manage other people's money for them, taking a percentage of the profits as a reward for good results. This is the route that great investors must take to win big – they must, in other words, combine their talent for stockmarket investing with the business of money management.

Stockmarket investing is not the only way to make a lot of money. In fact, it may not even be the best way. As Adam Smith points out in *The Money Game* (*see* pages 163–164), an owner/manager who builds a regular business to the point where it can be successfully floated on the stockmarket stands to make an enormous gain from the sale of his or her own shares to the public and may subsequently make more gains if the business continues to grow with the help of its much expanded capital base. It's horses for courses: I've included, amongst these 25 classics, one book, *Think Like a Tycoon*, to illustrate the important point that many people who achieve great wealth do so outside the stock market.

The majority of us, by the law of averages, will not take either route. This doesn't mean, however, that we cannot attain prosperity, security and financial comfort in our old age through investing. By prosperity I mean amassing a measly million dollars or two – perhaps more – in the course of a few decades of participation in the market, honestly, legally, and without taking crazy risks. The majority of investment books point out this simple fact and take pains to explain how, over the long-term, stock market investing has beat all other types of passive investment hands down. There may of course be periods in the future when this does not hold true, as there have been in the past (notably the 1930s) but so long as massive corporations continue to drive the economy, taxation is not too oppressive and the markets are run fairly and remain open to all, there is a strong probability that a long-term program of stock investing will produce better returns than can be obtained elsewhere.

The secret is to save. If you don't have much capital to start with, there is no alternative to this anyway. A regular program of investment in stocks, combined with the occasional addition of small lumps of capital when the markets are down, can bring you substantial wealth over half a century or so.

That's the good news. The bad news is that markets are driven by the psychological forces of fear and greed. As the economist Keynes (*see* pages 133–140) pointed out, "in the long run we are all dead." We'd like to enjoy our money when we're still relatively young. To make money more quickly we must take more risk. And the relationship of risk to reward is not necessarily clear cut; it's usually not possible to measure it accurately. We may think that a hot stock offers high rewards at low risk, for instance, but simply be wrong because we have based our judgement on imperfect information – and, believe it or not, in the stock market we almost always have imperfect information. Conversely, a stock which seems very risky – because it has a low capitalization, say, or because the market has taken against it – may turn out to be a strong performer for many years. It just isn't very easy to be successful when you try to take short cuts to the goal of large capital gains.

All the players in the market know about this uncertainty, and it makes them emotional in their decisions – which is sometimes called "investor psychology." *En masse*, investors in the markets behave almost neurotically, sometimes overvaluing companies and at other times undervaluing them. So, knowing these facts, how are we to approach investing? The 25 classics offer an array of solutions, not all equally convincing and many of which contradict one another. In the end, as *Punch* pointed out back in 1846, "You pays your money and you takes your choice." In this book I have tried to give an account of what the options are, as described in the books discussed. Like all investors, I have my own bias – I am not, for instance, enamored of technical analysis (*see* pages 203–208), nor am I convinced by the efficient market theory (*see* pages 181–183). For these opinions I make no apologies, for, as Mark Twain wrote, "it's difference of opinion that makes horse races" and so it is with the stock markets.

The authors of the 25 classics are not all "great investors." Some of them are journalists, like Edwin Lefèvre, author of *Reminiscences of a Stock Operator*, which is said to be based on the life of the famous speculator Jesse Livermore. Others are academics, like Burton Malkiel, author of the excellent *A Random Walk Down Wall Street* and the doughty J.K. Galbraith, whose history of the events of 1929, *The Great Crash 1929*, is featured here. Many of the books are old standards, like Benjamin Graham's *The Intelligent Investor*, while others are of recent date, but destined, I feel, for a long life, like Skidelsky's heavyweight biography *John Maynard Keynes*, and Kathryn Staley's gritty *The Art of Short Selling*.

There are quite a number of candidates for an investment book Hall of Fame that I haven't included at all, such as Graham and Dodd's *Security Analysis*, which is dull reading, or Peter

Lynch's *One Up on Wall Street* (I chose his more recent *Beating the Street* instead). There was also the problem of picking one book out of a series by or about a single investor. There is a plethora of books on Warren Buffett, for example, and I chose Roger Lowenstein's *Buffett, the Making of an American Capitalist* where I might equally as well have chosen *The Warren Buffett Way* by Robert G. Hagstrom Jr. Nor was it easy to choose which one of W.D. Gann's many volumes to represent his ideas.

In short, this has been an intentionally eclectic choice. If you are a fan of investment books, as I am, you'll know that there are many others that could have been, and perhaps ought to have been, included. But people who are starting out as investors need to begin somewhere, and I think my selection is broad enough and comprehensive enough to give plenty of food for thought. More experienced investors may have already read or heard of most of the 25 books covered here, but I hope that there are enough rare items to stimulate even their jaded appetites!

Use this book to familiarize yourself with the conflicting theories about how the markets work, to find out more about books you haven't read yet, and, perhaps, to rule out some as being not worth your time and trouble. Test your own intuitions and try to find your own personal investment style. After reading this volume you may decide to eschew direct investment in equities altogether, and stick to mutual funds, as many do with perfectly respectable results. Or maybe you'll decide to make your career in the financial markets. Perhaps you'll be stimulated by the accounts of derivatives trading in *Market Wizards* and *Trader Vic* to try your hand at the hectic game of futures trading. It's up to you. Whatever your circumstances and financial aspirations may be, I hope that you will find at least a few items of interest amongst these pages.

Another criterion I used in picking which books to examine was the sheer quality of their writing. Business books in general are not known for having great style, and many investment tomes make fairly dull reading despite the importance of the ideas they attempt to convey. Some, though, are a sheer delight to read, like Fred Schwed's charming *Where are the Customers' Yachts?*, which manages to convey through wit what others must hammer out by argument. A gem of a book such as this makes up for months of reading between the lines of the bland, slightly sinister, corporate-speak put out by so many companies and brokers and which, by osmosis, seems to affect otherwise quite useful investment books.

Investment is part of life, part of the extraordinary complexity and diversity within which we spend our days. The movement of stock prices, says John Train, is like an "encephalogram of the human race." I think he's right. This is, for me, what makes the stock markets so profoundly fascinating; they open up world upon world of human activity, and are truly history in the making.

Half a millennium of printed books has passed, in the Western world at least, and bibliophiles will know that throughout the period there have always been good books and bad books. Indeed, a bad book written centuries ago may be of great interest to us now because of what it unwittingly reveals about its own times. Two semi-fossils are covered here, the 17th-century *Confusión de Confusiones*, which is really quite a good book about an early stock market in Amsterdam, and the 19th-century *Extraordinary Popular Delusions and the Madness of Crowds*, which is a much-overrated potboiler that retells, inaccurately, the stories of three great booms and busts in Europe. Both are of interest to serious students of the markets, serving as a reminder, if any were needed, that investment is about human nature, and human judgements.

As I write this I am conscious that we may be in for some economic upheaval in the near future. The much vaunted economic miracle in parts of Asia has been unravelling for a year or more, and the Western markets appear overvalued and due for a "major correction" – that marvellous, mealy-mouthed euphemism for a bust. I expect the world to survive. While the US does remain the one great superpower, and therefore, if for no other reason, worthy of investors' attention, we should not forget that there is a "rest of the world" out there, full of interesting possibilities. Information technology has become a catalyst for globalization of the financial markets, and, in spite of the specter of new trade wars and tariff barriers, it seems likely that over the next few decades savvy investors will become increasingly internationalized.

Time will tell. In the meantime – and real life always happens "in the meantime" – don't worry too much about macroeconomics or bad news and concentrate on developing your own abilities as an investor. I hope that this book helps you do this.

Leo Gough, Singapore, 1998

AGAINST THE GODS
THE REMARKABLE STORY
OF RISK

by

Peter L. Bernstein

The word "risk" derives from the early Italian *risicare*, which means "to dare." In this sense, risk is a choice rather than a fate. The actions we dare to take, which depend on how free we are to make choices, are what the story of risk is all about. And that story helps define what it means to be a human being.

(Bernstein, page 8)

Material quoted within this chapter is extracted from *Against the Gods: the Remarkable Story of Risk* by Peter L. Bernstein, John Wiley & Sons, Inc., New York, 1996.

If you had bought a $10 ticket for a show and found, when you arrived at the theater, that you'd lost it, would you buy another one? If you had $20 in your pocket and intended to purchase a ticket when you arrived at the theater, would you still buy one if you found that you had lost $10 when you got there? If you have an extremely good month trading stocks, are you more likely or less likely to obtain above-average returns in the following month? Is it riskier to invest across a wide range of emerging markets than to stick to the S&P 500?

These are just a few of the apparently simple questions that modern explorers of risk use to discover hitherto unrecognized aspects of this extraordinary, multi-dimensional phenomenon. You might think that the rules of risk-assessment had all been figured out a long time ago, but in fact our understanding of it is still developing. Risk management has practical applications in many fields, from war to engineering, but it is in the financial markets that we see the problems in their most naked form.

The truth is that human beings are not born knowing all there is to know about risk. Our ability to deal with it, and to make appropriate decisions regarding it, has to be developed – this is something that we have to learn and improve upon throughout our lives. There are many ambiguities: as individuals, the "right choices" depend a great deal upon our circumstances. For instance, it makes more sense for someone with no financial assets to take great risks in attempting to acquire them than for an extremely wealthy person to take great risks in attempting to acquire more wealth, because the potential rewards will confer less real benefits to the wealthy person.

Against the Gods is an extremely useful book for anyone interested in gaining a better understanding of this fascinating aspect of life. In particular, it helps us not to attempt to reinvent the wheel – many of our "crude intuitions" about risk have been analyzed and refined by generations of thinkers, and the book provides, in an accessible form, a clear explanation of the essential ideas and techniques.

The book is a history of risk from about 1200 A.D. to the present. It has been much acclaimed and here, perhaps for the first time, we can see the way that Western ideas have developed over the centuries, their utility and their inadequacies. It is also up-to-date, at the time of writing anyway, and this is important because we appear to be living at a time where significant progress is being made in the understanding of this mysterious topic.

Against the Gods is a useful potted history of risk from about 1200 AD to the present day. The book has been much acclaimed – perhaps a little too much, since there is little that is original in the book and much which has been covered better elsewhere. It is, however, up-to-date, and this is important because we appear to be living at a time where significant progress is being made in the understanding of this mysterious topic.

For Bernstein, the serious work begins after 1200, although the first chapter, entitled "To 1200: Beginnings," does go back even further into the history of risk. Unfortunately, this chapter has to cover so much ground so quickly that it cannot really do such a vast stretch of history justice – much of it being of the "First there was the Big Bang; then the dinosaurs came" variety. It does make some useful points, though, as it briefly discusses why the ancient Greeks, despite their love of reason and proof, did not do much work on risk, the importance of the invention of the zero and the adoption of Hindu/Arabic numerals in the West.

For the author though, this period was clearly only a warm-up for the main event: the modern study of risk. In the introduction the author says that "the revolutionary idea that defines the boundary between modern times and the past is the mastery of risk;" a bold statement indeed, and one which is open to question. The ancients were not as dumb as books like this would lead us to believe, but that question is broad enough to be the subject of many lifetimes' worth of study, so perhaps we can't blame Bernstein for concentrating his efforts on the more recent, and more documented breakthroughs in our struggle with risk.

Until quite modern times, much of the serious work on risk arose from the needs of those spiritual cousins of investors, gamblers. In the 1500s, for instance, a physician and inveterate gambler named Cardano wrote a useful book on playing dice which is "the first known effort to put measurement at the service of risk." Within 100 years of his death all the major problems in probability analysis had been solved. "The next step," writes Bernstein, "was to tackle the question of how human beings recognize and respond to the problems they confront."

In response, he goes on to recount the life of Blaise Pascal, the French mathematician who made great contributions to what was to become decision theory. Pascal had a friend, Chevalier de Mère, who was a gambler who had adopted such interesting betting tactics as playing often, with a large amount of capital, with the aim of making small profits over time. Together with the mathematician Fermat, Pascal devised ways of analyzing probable outcomes using the famous "Pascal's triangle" and other methods.

A few years later, in 1662, a self-taught British tradesman, John Graunt, published a groundbreaking book, *Natural and Political Observations made upon the Bills of Mortality*. The book used the raw data of births and deaths recorded in London from 1604 to 1661 and made great strides in the application of statistical sampling. In it he established some important principles of statistical analysis, such as the problems of getting accurate data, and how to estimate the average likely outcome (in this case, of life expectancy). Then came the famous coffee house of Lloyd's, where the insurance of shipping began; it's still operating today as the world's most famous name in insurance, despite problems in the late 1980s, out of a vast high-rise in the City of London.

As the book reaches more recent times, the discoveries it discusses become more challenging. One of the most important ideas, from the point of view of investors, is the regression to the mean, discovered by Sir Francis Galton, a relative of Charles Darwin. Galton found when measuring groups of things that they tended to fall in a distinct pattern, a bell-shaped curve or "normal distribution." Most of the things measured tended to fall in the bulge of the curve, with fewer of them tailing off at the extremes at either end. Examining sweetpeas, he found that the offspring of individual sweetpeas tended to be normally distributed (by weight and size) and that they also tended to become more average, overall than their parents: in other words, the offspring of large or small parents were, on average, closer to the mean size of sweetpeas overall – the "regression to the mean." The same was true, he found, of the height of human parents and their children.

Bernstein rightly makes much of this phenomenon. He describes a 1986 study that showed that countries which had the lowest levels of industrial productivity, in 1870, have had the highest in more recent years, while the opposite is true of countries that had the highest productivity in 1870. Rich and powerful countries, like the US, have had their high periods of growth and are now slowing down. Furthermore, the difference between the growth rates of countries is converging – from 8:1 in 1870 to only 2:1 today. Bernstein points out that the doomsayers in the US who deplore "what they allege to be a slowdown in productivity growth over the past quarter-century" are missing this point, since "each successive technological miracle counts for less as the base from which we measure gets bigger."

So are we simply fated to end up near the average in the long run? Bernstein says that regression to the mean is only a tool and should not be turned into a religion. He quotes Galton as saying, "An Average is but a solitary fact, whereas if a single other fact be added to it, an entire Normal Scheme, which nearly corresponds to the observed one, starts potentially into existence." This appears to mean that there is not necessarily one long continuous mean; things may happen that radically alter a system so that a new "average" begins. Bernstein gives two examples of how one can over-rely on regression to the mean. First, when President Herbert Hoover said in 1930 that prosperity was just around the corner – he was right, but several years too soon, and he failed to predict the intensification of the Great Depression that came in between. Second, when in 1959 stock prices continued to soar despite the fact that their yields were lower than bonds – which had never happened before. At the time experienced investors could still remember the crash of 1929 and were convinced that stock prices would regress to a mean that they understood – instead, stock prices continued to climb.

"Once you become sensitized to it, you see regression everywhere," says Princeton-based Israeli psychologist Daniel Kahneman, co-inventor of Prospect Theory which deals with the way people make mistakes when they are faced with decisions involving risk. If you perform extremely well on one day, it's quite likely you won't do so well on the next, and *vice versa*. Prospect Theory also has interesting insights into "risk aversion," the idea that people don't like to take risks when they have the chance of certainty. According to Prospect Theory, it is not that people are risk averse, it is that they are "loss averse" – they are more sensitive to negative stimuli than positive ones, which leads to them being, on average, less and less willing to take risks with their money the richer they get. This could explain why financial institutions take fewer risks in the market than the little guys, and why you don't find many people with inherited wealth playing for high stakes in the commodity markets. As one of Bernstein's clients told him, "Remember, young man, you don't have to make me rich. I'm rich already."

Much of the newest work on risk takes entirely different approaches than the linear, rational tradition we've inherited from the ancient Greeks *via* the Renaissance. Chaos theory, for instance, rejects the normal distribution; the world is in a state of flux, but all events have their causes, even if we aren't able to perceive them. The theory, however, has not accomplished much in the practical sphere, says Bernstein. The Black–Scholes model, on the other hand, has revolutionized the world of derivatives by providing a better way of measuring their risk using a complex method based on four elements: prices, interest rates, time and volatility. This approach was rapidly adopted in the futures markets after it was published in 1970, and today we see that financial institutions and large companies are very active in derivatives trading – for hedging purposes only, they allege, but a few widely publicized disasters, such as the bankruptcy of Orange County, California and the collapse of the British merchant bank, Barings, suggest that some people are being too smart for their own good.

For investors, *Against the Gods* is a good starting-off point if you know nothing about risk; it gives you a wide-ranging and generally accurate survey of most, if not all, the really important discoveries and explains them in a clear and understandable way. Even if you hate math, you will be able to follow these ideas; as Socrates pointed out more than two millennia ago, you can come to understand the most subtle and complicated things, so long as you approach them in the right way.

This remarkable story of risk will arm you with no practical tools or formulas, but the journey will leave you with a better understanding of, and respect for, the nature of risk. This book is one for the bedside table – dip into it each night, and let your unconscious work on it while you're asleep!

THE ART OF
SHORT SELLING

by

Kathryn F. Staley

ZZZZ Best, whiz kid Barry Minkow's hot-growth company, had a market value of $200 million in the spring of
1987. Business was great for the company, and they
announced a contract to clean two large buildings in
Sacramento for $8 million. Carpet-cleaning competitors
told Feshbach analysts that the two largest cleaning contracts to date (the MGM Grand and the Las Vegas Hilton)
capped at a price of $3.5 million, so the Feshbachs smelled
a skunk, started looking, and shorted aggressively. The
stock price rallied despite rumors of false billing in late
May of 1987. By July, ZZZZ Best was bankrupt. In March
1989, the amazing Minkow was sentenced to 25 years for
fraud: no contracts, no revenues, and a money-laundering
scheme. The Feshbachs, meanwhile, went home happy
and richer.

(Staley, pages 43–44)

Material quoted within this chapter is extracted from *The Art of Short Selling*
by Kathryn F. Staley, John Wiley & Sons, Inc., New York, 1997.

Short selling is centuries older than the stock markets, yet it has always had a bad press. There seems to be something unsporting in betting that a stock or commodity will go down when everyone else has bet that it is going up, and short sellers have been blamed for everything from the South Sea Bubble to the 1929 Wall Street Crash. Napoleon Bonaparte thought that short sellers were traitors. More recently, the 1997 currency crisis in Asia evoked a whirlwind of abuse from some politicians in the affected countries, most notably from Malaysia's Dr Mahathir, who conducted a very public campaign against currency traders who had sold the region's currencies short, singling out George Soros (*see* pages 193–201) as the prime culprit, as had British politicians some years earlier when Soros and others made money betting that sterling would fall out of the European Union's Exchange Rate Mechanism (ERM).

Welcome to a secret, quite beautiful world. Kathryn Staley tells us that there are only 10 or 15 people in the US who are full-time professional short sellers practicing "fundamental, information-based, non-computer motivated short selling." Many people and organizations sell short sometimes and there are a number of dedicated short selling funds, although few of these stay in business for long.

What's it all about? To sell common stock short in the US, you borrow it from a broker to sell it in the market. You put up 50 percent of the short-sale price (a Federal Reserve rule). The broker obtains the stock from customer margin accounts or another broker.

On the NYSE, NASDAQ and AMEX, the stock price must move up before a short sale is allowed. Once the transaction is made, the broker calculates the gain or loss on a daily or weekly basis. If the price of the stock moves down, the short seller is winning; if the price moves up, he or she must put up more money for margin. When you decide to close the position, you buy the stock and deliver it to the broker.

There are two main risks in short selling, first, that the stock price goes up, forcing you to deposit more money with the broker, and second, that the lender of the stock wants it back.

This is a painful risk – the broker has the right to ask you for the stock if the owner needs it (remember that short sellers "borrow" the stock). In such a case you must buy the stock at the current market price – known as a "buy-in."

A "buy-in" can be disastrous. If you sell a small company short, its small "float" of shares (the number of shares in issue which are not owned by insiders or holders with a stake of more than 5 percent of the company) makes you especially vulnerable, so many short sellers stick to stocks with capitalizations of more than $500 million. As a percentage of the total market, short selling is tiny – only 1.3 percent of the NYSE in 1997.

Kathryn Staley is a succinct writer who obviously loves this business. For her, professional short selling is all about fundamental analysis – it's a numbers game where you have to do your sums and your thinking very carefully indeed. The main problem for short sellers, she says, is being right too soon – you may be correct in your belief that a company is grossly overvalued, but it may take much longer than you expect for the stock price to actually drop. In the meantime you may be hard pressed by margin calls and you are continually at risk of a forced "buy-in."

The book gives a seven-point approach for examining short sale candidates:

1. The search for problem companies – negative articles in established periodicals such as *Barron's* and *Forbes* may trigger a drop in the stock price. The *Wall Street Journal* publishes data on short positions, and "middle-sized" short positions in companies which are not candidates for a buy-out or have convertible common stock are promising since a professional short seller has already taken a position, but if it is very high (above 15 percent of the share float in the 1990s) then, says Staley, buy-ins are likely.

   Other useful areas to look at are industries that are particularly vulnerable to fraud and or financial manipulation, such as franchises, real estate and financial services.

2. Examine the financial statements that all listed companies must file with the Securities and Exchange Commission (who provide detailed information on what is required in each of their multiplicity of forms) – obtain the last six 10Qs, the last two 10Ks, proxies, annuals and any 8Ks. This gives enough

data to analyze the last two years' performance in inventories, receivables and margins by quarter and three years of annual figures. Staley gives detailed help on how to analyze these figures but those new to company accounts may first need to study a book such as *Financial Statement Analysis* by Leopold Bernstein.

Essentially, the approach is first to see if there is "anything funny about the numbers," then to apply all the standard ratios, examine the cashflow statement and the description of the business and finally to mentally relate the three main financial statements (balance sheet, income statement and cashflow statement) together to see how they mesh. This task does require accounting skills but, as Staley points out, experience as a businessperson helps more than "analyst acumen." What you are attempting to discover is whether or not the business is really as it superficially appears to be.

3. As those of us who invest in foreign markets (all of which are less well-regulated) are well aware, the SEC, for all its bureaucratic faults, provides a boon to investors in the vast amount of information that it requires from listed companies. Key documents to examine are:

- **Form 144** – records stock sales by key officers of the company and is filed on the day of the sale.
- **Form 4** – a list of sales and purchases of stocks by key officers, filed 10 days after the end of the month in which their positions changed.

- **13-D** – records any position of 5 percent or more in the company within 10 days of the purchase.
- **Proxy statements** – Staley says this is the "best of all sources." Among other things, it gives details of stock owned by the management, their salaries and employment contracts (including stock options), pending lawsuits and numerous other important matters.

Here, the short seller is looking for signs of greed and misbehavior on the part of insiders, such as: excessive bonuses and salaries in relation to their competitors; business dealings with relatives of the officers; too-generous loans to key insiders. Any of these may indicate that the managers are enriching themselves at the expense of the shareholders.

4. Next, review the industry that the company is in, its competitors and its customers. Use the form 10K as a basis from which to start. Compare such items as profit margins, inventory sizes and growth rates with those of listed competitors. Then visit one of the company's stores or offices to see if the reality matches the paper picture.

5. Follow the way that big holdings are traded, in particular the activities of the financial institutions. Staley says that high institutional ownership can be a good sign for shorts, since they can pull out fast if the news is bad – an interesting twist to the conventional idea that institutional ownership makes for safety and stability!

6. Get analysts' reports on the company for the information they

provide, not for their opinions. Use *Forbes* and *Barron's* who, she says, are more likely than analysts to report bad news.

7. Once you've done the preliminary work you may decide not to short the stock. Keep abreast of developments, though, because it may be worthwhile shorting in a year or two. Conversely, if you have gone short on a stock because of certain factors which are corrected later by the company, close your position and accept defeat.

Sounds like hard work? It is. But most successful investors agree that you have to work for your money in the market. Don't let the complexities of the foregoing discourage you from reading this book – most of the text consists of entertaining case studies of real companies which were shorted, and how the short-sellers fared.

Crazy Eddie

My favorite case study in this book is the story of Crazy Eddie, a company which in 1986 owned 24 consumer electronics stores in and around New York. Analysis by short sellers found numerous negative factors, including the following.

- The share price had moved from $4.50 in 1984 to $37.50 in the second half of 1986, with a 41 percent institutional ownership. The company looked "a little overpriced" and Wall Street was evidently counting on growth.

- A large number of close relatives of the founder, Eddie Antar, were officers of the company, enjoying generous salaries and stock option plans.

- The company traded closely with a corporation owned by close relatives and made loans to several other family-owned entities including a medical school in the Caribbean. The company had made numerous interest-free loans to individual family members.

- Profits after tax were low at 5 percent of sales.

- Although it was turning over a large amount of goods, the company had no computerized inventory accounting systems.

- The price/earnings ratio in early 1986 was high at 39.

- During the year, the management received a large number of new stock options, effectively diluting the earnings per share figure.

- By October, the stock had dropped after a two for one stock split to $15.25, a 15 percent slide from the $37.50 price earlier in the year.

In January 1987 the stock dropped by $1.375 to $9.875. Eddie Antar announced his resignation. At this point many short sellers closed their positions; if they'd sold short at the highest price in 1986, they would now have made an excellent profit. Other short sellers waited for more.

The price continued to slide until May, when Eddie Antar returned to bid $7 per share for the whole company. He was topped by a rival bid of $8. The market price moved back to $8. In June the SEC announced that it was instituting an inquiry. A 10K was filed revealing a number of problems, including lawsuits and a doubling of Eddie Antar's salary to $600,000 which he continued to receive despite his resignation. In August Antar dropped his bid and the share price dropped to $3.50. In November, new managers announced that $45 million of inventory was missing, a figure which later grew to $65 million. Eddie Antar went on the run having allegedly hidden $60 million dollars (about the size of the inventory loss) abroad. He "surrendered to US marshals" in 1990. The new management claimed that Antar had falsified inventory and profit accounts and destroyed records in order to inflate the reported assets of the company. Crazy Eddie finally filed for bankruptcy in 1989.

Short selling doesn't depend on discovering crooks – there are plenty of companies to sell short which are merely badly managed and over-hyped – but there must be a special satisfaction to be had from making huge profits (a possible 90 percent return in under a year in the case of Crazy Eddie) by spotting a fraud long before the rest of the world even suspects a problem.

3

BARBARIANS AT THE GATE

THE FALL OF RJR NABISCO

by

**Bryan Burrough
and John Helyar**

Yet in the world's greatest concentration of RJR share-holders – Winston-Salem, North Carolina – few were thanking Johnson even as money gushed into town. Nearly $2 billion of checks arrived in the late-February mail. Now, more than ever, Winston-Salem was the city of reluctant millionaires. Local brokers, and bankers got calls from distraught clients. "I won't sell my stock," one sobbed. "Daddy said don't ever sell the RJR stock." They were patiently told that they had to. They were told the world had changed.

(Burrough and Helyar, page 617)

Material quoted within this chapter is extracted from *Barbarians at the Gate: The Fall of RJR Nabisco* by Bryan Burrough and John Helyar, Arrow Books, London, 1990.

This is the story of the battle for control of RJR Nabisco, a classic tale of 1980s greed. These two industrial giants, both producers of many household-name brands, had not long been merged when their new CEO decided to attempt a leveraged buy-out (LBO). Nothing wrong in that, on the face of it, but the times, and conditions within the company, make it more of a story of a rape than of a constructive deal. While senior executives were living high on the hog, investment bankers, intoxicated with their increasing success, began to circle like vultures. Perhaps the story is best summarized by one former RJR Nabisco employee, who described it thus:

> "Imagine you lived in this great old house. You grew up in it, and all of your happy memories are in it, and you take special care of it for the next generation. Then one day, you come home to discover it's been turned into a brothel. That's how I feel about RJR.
>
> *(page 63)*

Employees of RJR's core tobacco-manufacturing business in Winston-Salem, North Carolina, many of whom were substantial stockholders, were particularly disturbed by the LBO battle – many saw it as a forced sale by outsiders of an inheritance that was, in a real sense, their whole lives.

The complexity and legal dangers of recounting such a complicated series of events presents great difficulties for any author. Yet this story had to be told – controversy rages over whether LBOs are good for a company – and how the benefits should be defined – but it is rare for investors to get a chance to follow a blow-by-blow account of the events as they occurred and to obtain an insight into the characters involved. *Barbarians at the Gate* is a must-read for private investors who don't have much experience of how the upper echelons of the corporate and banking worlds sometimes operate and for this reason it is a classic. Unfortunately, it is also one of the worst-written business books of all time. This makes life hard on the reader, who must struggle for the meat of the story through pages peppered with such masterpieces of irrelevance as: "Sunday evening Ted Forstmann was at his East River apartment enduring a vigorous rubdown from a masseur once employed by the Italian national tennis team."

The authors, reporters for *The Wall Street Journal*, state in their introduction that their goal "in pursuing the story behind these public events has been to meet the standard of accuracy and general excellence that the *Journal* sets for journalists everywhere." Accurate it may be, but generally excellent it ain't. They have stuffed a vast amount of facts into their book, based on over 100 interviews, and have chosen to cast it in pseudo-thriller form – hence the half-hearted effort to add color to this ugly story about ugly people by such devices as pointless descriptions of where the characters are when they take phone calls. This is an idiot-savant approach to what is a real problem. Unraveling the complexities of what was the biggest attempted leveraged buy-out (LBO) of all time is not easy. To create drama, the authors have their affectless characters drone banal reconstructed dialogue: "'Speaking as an adviser, and I'm an adviser now,' Boisi said, 'I have a thought. I want you to tell them that you're upset. I mean it. We need to tell them we didn't like what happened in there.'" (Page 346.) Maybe this kind of thing works in a movie, but it doesn't work over 600 pages of text.

This is a pity, because for investors the RJR Nabisco story is important. Takeovers, mergers and buy-outs are usually excellent news for the stockholders, since the price paid is often far in excess of the market price. Many studies have shown that such deals are frequently too rich and end up hurting the companies in the long-term. The purchaser takes on vast debt to make the deal, and the company is then burdened with massive repayments. For this reason, private investors are often well-advised to take their profits at the time of the deal and leave others to suffer the consequences.

Why are companies bought for too much money? Mergers and acquisitions are surrounded by controversy – the benefits of the potential advantages, such as perceived "synergies" and cost savings, are material for acrimonious debate. What is clear, however, is that in many deals certain players may benefit hugely whatever the ultimate fate of the merged company. They are the investment bankers, who act as middle men and enjoy vast fees from a successful outcome; the lenders, who get to lend large sums on good security; the management, who may receive an overgenerous cut from the deal; and the purchaser, who assumes power. *Barbarians at the Gate* recounts one of the grossest examples of this type of corporate plundering in recent times.

At the heart of it all was Ross Johnson, the CEO of RJR Nabisco. Johnson, a Canadian, had worked his way up the ladder through expertly playing corporate politics, moving from company to company in a relatively undistinguished career until he became the president of the Canadian arm of Standard Brands, a US company. Johnson rose to this challenge by applying a strategy of perpetual restructuring – a type of "divide and rule" approach which he had used before – at the head of a picked team of managers whose loyalty he ensured by a combination of charm, lavish generosity and late-night drinking sessions. By 1976 Johnson was heir apparent to the CEO. In a confrontation over expense-account violations, Johnson won the board's support and ousted his boss, achieving his ambition of heading an NYSE-listed company.

In 1981 in a $1.9 billion stock swap, Standard Brands merged with the much larger Nabisco Brands. Nabisco, a century old, was a vast concern that owned such famous food products as Oreo cookies and Ritz crackers.

Following the merger Johnson was made president. He soon chafed at Nabisco's staid ways and began to outmaneuver the CEO by encouraging him to loosen the purse strings on executive salaries. Gradually, Johnson engineered the replacement of top executives by his own managers from Standard Brands. By 1984 he was CEO.

Then in 1985 Nabisco merged with the paternalistic tobacco company RJ Reynolds, makers of Camel cigarettes. Based in Winston-Salem, North Carolina, RJ Reynolds was a deeply conservative company with a boss who wanted to turn it into a giant (it had already swallowed companies such as Del Monte and Kentucky Fried Chicken).

Once again Johnson was heading the smaller company and once again he was able to win the support of the board, oust the CEO and supplant the directors with his own loyal men from Standard Brands. He now headed the 19th largest industrial company in the USA. Playing the games of power masterfully, Johnson moved the corporate HQ from Winston-Salem to Atlanta to weaken his enemies in RJ Reynolds and allow himself to be courted by investment bankers.

In 1988 he decided to attempt a leveraged buy-out (LBO). If successful, he and others would receive huge wealth as part of the deal and get more control over the company into the bargain. If he failed, he would still have his $50+ million golden parachute for a soft landing.

In the late 1980s LBOs were in fashion, but they were dangerous for the managers who initiated them, since bids from third parties could appear which, if successful, often meant mass executive sackings. Johnson was gambling that the company was just too big for any group to attempt an unfriendly bid.

Barbarians at the Gate laboriously details the hectic months that followed; rival bids did appear and an intense battle ensued, ultimately leaving Henry Kravis, an LBO artist, as the effective owner of RJR Nabisco. A sum of some $25 billion was paid to the shareholders, $18.9 billion of it in cash. This money caused spikes in the nation's money-supply statistics as it poured through the banking system to its stunned recipients.

From the point of view of the small private investor, LBOs are generally good news. If someone wants to pay you way more for your stock than it is actually worth, why complain? This was a point that Ross Johnson frequently made to justify his own position; in a bidding race for a company, the stockholders can sit back happily as the value of their holdings soar. Yet there is something a little worrying about such short termist views. Mergers and acquisitions activity is at its highest at the top of bull markets, when it becomes easy for specialists to borrow the vast sums needed to gain control of corporations. Whether or not such purchases are beneficial to the company concerned is often not clear until years afterwards, by which time the individuals concerned may have moved on, in some cases remaining entirely unaccountable for their actions. As the book's title suggests, the instincts behind LBOs are more than a little like those of the barbarian hordes that hovered around the edges of the crumbling Roman empire, waiting for internal decadence to leave an unguarded opening.

Read it and weep.

BEATING THE DOW

by
Michael O'Higgins
with John Downes

In 1985, Texaco, America's third largest oil company, was ordered to pay Pennzoil Company a huge $10.3 billion judgment. In 1987, Texaco filed for bankruptcy. Its stock plunged 28 percent to $27 per share. In 1989, with the legal claim settled, a post-bankruptcy share of a restructured Texaco has since gone even higher.

When deadly gas leaked from a pesticide plant in Bhopal, India, killing over 3300 people and injuring thousands more, Union Carbide Corporation, America's third largest chemical company and owner of 51 percent of the plant, was sued for over $3 billion. Its stock sank 21 percent to $11, but it bounced back in 1985. In 1989, the Bhopal litigation settled, Union Carbide shares hit an adjusted all-time high of $33 before entering an industry downcycle.

By virtue of their sheer size and strength – call it raw staying power – blue chip companies tend to be survivors. The old adage "the bigger they are, the harder they fall" doesn't hold when you are talking about corporate giants.

(O'Higgins, pages 3 and 4)

Material quoted within this chapter is extracted from *Beating the Dow* by Michael O'Higgins with John Downes, HarperCollins, New York, 1992. Part of this chapter originally appeared in *Portfolio Management* by Leo Gough (Fleet Street Publications Ltd, 1998) and is reprinted here by kind permission of the publishers.

It is easy to overcomplicate things in life – especially activities such as investment where there is far more information available than a single individual can ever hope to absorb. When it comes to market information, the "signal to noise" ratio is low – so investors must discriminate. But if you're just starting out, how do you know what to ignore and what to investigate? In such a complex world, how can a beginner keep stock selection simple enough to handle?

In *Beating the Dow*, Michael O'Higgins, a Wall Street investment manager, provides an answer to this dilemma: stick to blue chips. In fact, stick exclusively to the 30 stocks that make up the Dow Jones Industrial Average (DJIA), he says, and you can get all the upside you could ever want.

Of course, if you believe the random walkers such as Malkiel (*see* pages 175–183), then no stock investment system can work indefinitely but O'Higgins' system (known technically as a "relative strength" system) is certainly credible in present conditions – in essence, it exploits the inflexibility of the huge institutional funds that make up, in cash terms, most of the market and which tend to move in predictable ways. It is not inconceivable that at some time in the future you might fail when using the O'Higgins method because the structure of the market had subtly – or not so subtly – changed. For the time being, though, it seems promising.

The system is conservative, mechanical and workable. Since you trade only once a year, it doesn't take up much of your time.

Believe it or not, these are major points in its favor – when you are starting out, it takes time to get used the idea of actually owning a stock, time to familiarize yourself with all the sources of financial information and time to realize that your friends and relatives almost certainly don't know what they are talking about when it comes to investments. If you work for a living, this basic process can easily take years, since you'll be doing it on evenings and weekends.

Perhaps it should take this long; investors in the looking-glass world of the stock market must unlearn many popular prejudices. Many people feel that direct investment in equities is too difficult for them and end up buying mutual funds – a conservative decision, perhaps, but an expensive and ultimately unsatisfactory one. By using the O'Higgins method you can gain experience in direct equity investment at relatively low risk, and, since it is a mechanical method, you don't have to be knowledgeable about stock analysis.

So, why the stocks of the Dow Jones Industrial Average (DJIA)? First, O'Higgins points out that all its constituents are multinationals and that together their turnover exceeds the GNPs of *all* countries except the USA and Japan. They are vast, sound enterprises that are unlikely to broke. Secondly, as they are the most widely and publicly analyzed of all stocks, it is possible for the inexperienced investor to get to know them well.

In the first part of the book O'Higgins sets out the basic rationale of the system. In the second part he goes on to discuss the companies in some detail. At the time of the 1992 edition, the constituents of the DJIA were:

Code	Company name	Code	Company name
AA	Alcoa	JNJ	Johnson & Johnson
ALD	Allied Signal	JPM	JP Morgan Bank
AXP	American Express	KO	Coca-Cola
BA	Boeing	MCD	McDonalds
CAT	Caterpillar	MMM	Minnesota Mining and Manufacturing (3M)
CHV	Chevron	MO	Philip Morris
DD	Du Pont	MRK	Merck
DIS	Disney	PG	Procter and Gamble
EK	Eastman Kodak	S	Sears, Roebuck
GE	General Electric	T	AT&T
GM	General Motors	TRV	Travelers Group
GT	Goodyear Tire	UK	Union Carbide
HWP	Hewlett-Packard	UTX	United Technologies
IBM	International Business Machines	WMT	WalMart Stores
IP	International Paper	XON	Exxon

Some of the names may be unfamiliar to new investors, but who hasn't heard of Coca-Cola, Disney or IBM? Most of us encounter these companies in the day-to-day business of our own lives and, as their customers, we already have some sense of their performance.

As with other indices, companies are occasionally substituted for others, either because a company runs into problems which reduces its financial strength, or because the compilers of the index want to make it more representative of the changing nature of the economy as a whole. O'Higgins says that, for the 50 years up to the publication of his book, two-thirds of the companies had not changed.

This is important because you can make mistakes with indices that are always changing their constituents – some of the emerging market indices are doing this all the time, a reflection of the volatile regions they are dealing with. The make-up of the DJIA, on the other hand, is very stable.

O'Higgins continues with a series of three-page discussions of each of the 30 stocks in the DJIA, together with a chart of each one's performance from the mid-1970s to 1990. He contrives to make them interesting, and thereby does his readers a great service; as an investor, you need to start getting to know the big companies and what they do and to understand the markets in which they operate. It is clear that O'Higgins understands some of the companies less well than the others – you can tell he has a manufacturing bent and finds it easier to write about companies that make "real" things, as opposed to, say, banks, whose balance sheets are easier to disguise and whose businesses are more difficult to understand. His description of the bank JP Morgan, for instance, is not one of the book's stronger chapters.

Beating the Dow goes on to describe the ups and downs in the US market during the last few decades. It's an oft-told story of fads and fashions succeeding one another as innovations fueled wild speculation. In the 1960s, for instance, at the height of the confidence in economic growth and worldwide enthusiasm for the space race, any company with "tronics" in its name seemed to attract investors' money, even if it had nothing to do with technology. In the 1970s, following the first oil crisis brought about by the newly powerful OPEC, institutional money focused on blue chips – the "nifty 50" – driving their price earnings ratios as high as 100 times annual earnings, which is a level that is impossible for stocks to sustain for long before dropping. In the 1980s the craze was for mergers, with many companies buying others in what ultimately turned out to be lousy deals for the purchasers. More recent trends include the craze for biotechnology and genetic engineering. The basic point that O'Higgins makes, as have many other investment writers, is that such fads are relatively short-lived and their followers are likely to lose heavily when the fad finally evaporates and the hot stocks plunge.

The basic method

O'Higgins describes several ways of investing in DJIA companies, all of which have done well historically (of, course, this doesn't guarantee that they will do as well in the future). The basic method goes like this.

1. Draw up a table with five columns.

2. From the financial pages of newspapers such as the *Wall Street Journal* or the *New York Times*, copy out the list of the DJIA companies in alphabetical order.

3. In the next column, fill in the closing prices that day for each company.

4. In the next column, list the yields for each company.

5. Look down the list of yields and highlight the ten highest; if there are two with the same yield, pick the one with the lower closing price. In the next column, rank these ten companies, giving the one with the highest yield "1" and the one with the lowest yield "10."

6. Now invest an equal amount of money in each of the ten shares.

7. Do nothing for exactly 12 months.

8. When 12 months are up, list the new closing prices for your ten stocks. To work out your return on each one, subtract the price you actually bought it at from the new closing price and add in any dividends.

9. Add up all the returns and divide the total by the number of stocks (which is ten) to get the return on your portfolio. Compare this figure with the change in the DJIA for the 12 months.

10. Now go back to step 1 and repeat the process to select the ten highest yielding stocks. Sell any stocks in your current portfolio which aren't in the new list, and purchase the others.

That's all you have to do! Year in, year out, just keep on doing it. For the period which O'Higgins examines, which is 18.5 years from 1973 to 30 of June 1990, he shows that this method produced an overall return (not inflation adjusted) of 1753.14 percent, compared with the DJIA's 559.31 percent. During that time there were only three years when it didn't beat the Dow, and only three years when it produced a negative return.

Taking on more risk

O'Higgins shows that if you picked the five highest-yielding and lowest-priced stocks, you'd have done even better during the same period (a result of 2819.41 percent). This is somewhat riskier than investing in ten stocks, since you have less diversification.

He then examines an even riskier method – just picking the high-yielding stock of the ten which is the second-lowest-priced (not the lowest-priced). Using the same method as before, you hold the stock for 12 months and then switch to the new stock which fits the criteria (or keep the same stock if that is the one that fits). This method produced, in the same 18.5 year period, a stunning return of 6245.49 percent.

The reason why O'Higgins recommends picking the second-lowest-priced stock, rather than the lowest, is because he believes that the lowest-priced stock is likely to be in trouble and thus may not produce such good returns.

A system to beat the Dow?

The efficient marketeer academics, remember, will say that while it may have worked for the period which O'Higgins examined, it is unlikely to work over the very long-term. O'Higgins does not explicitly address this criticism; in my own opinion, the efficient marketeers are almost certainly correct, but this may not invalidate the system over the next few years.

Here, briefly, is O'Higgin's explanation for why he thinks the system works.

- Yield is simply the dividend per stock as a percentage of a company's market capitalization and is a standard measure. Dividends are considered to be very important, and large companies will go to great lengths to keep paying out their dividends. They are prevented by law from doing this from their capital – it has to come out of the profits they make from their business each year.

- A high yield implies that a company's stock is relatively unpopular – if there were a strong demand for the stock the price would go up, automatically making the yield go down if the dividend remained the same because it would be a smaller percentage of the stock market value of the company (the market capitalization).

- DJIA dividends are fairly secure, and account for 40 to 50 percent of the total return obtained from DJIA companies. This is the reason for picking high yielders!

O'Higgins claims that lower-priced blue chips have a more

volatile price range than do the higher-priced ones. By picking the lowest-priced high yielders, the system attempts to increase the chances of seeing a big price rise each year.

Does the system work on foreign exchanges?

Non-US nationals can purchase DJIA stocks and apply the O'Higgins system, although they will be at a slight disadvantage to US investors, because they are likely to incur additional expenses for dealing in overseas stocks, such as higher commissions and dividend-handling fees. Tax breaks in their own countries may not apply – for instance, UK residents cannot hold US stocks in the PEP or ISA schemes. There is also the risk that the dollar may strengthen against the investor's home currency. For all these reasons, the return may not be as good. Some work has been done to test if the O'Higgins system works in the UK; although you can't rely on dividends from blue chips in the UK in the way you can in the US, various studies suggest that if you apply the method to the FTSE 100 (not the FT 30), you will also get above average returns.

The verdict

This system is conservative, since it only invests in blue chips, which are unlikely to go bust. The numbers are persuasive, and the arguments about yields and prices are not particularly controversial.

The benefit of this method for the outright beginner is that it simply removes the difficult problem of choosing and monitoring stocks. The O'Higgins system allows you to avoid choice paralysis and information overload by keeping it simple and focusing on a small number of highly visible, widely reported blue chip stocks.

One of the main ways that stockbrokers make money from inexperienced private clients is advising them on the latest hot prospect. By sticking rigidly to this method, if only for a few years, you will avoid all the temptation to fool around with stocks in companies you don't know and don't understand. Naturally, the performance of DJIA stocks are also subject to market vagaries and changes in their own fortunes, but at least they are massively rich and powerful organizations that are unlikely to go broke – which may well not be true of a hot tip you have been given by someone.

O'Higgins comes across as a sincere and balanced individual; he's not system-obsessed. The data and arguments in his book are well-founded – while, as ever, there's no guarantee that the method will succeed in the future, beginner investors could certainly do a lot worse than giving it a five-year trial.

BEATING
THE STREET

by
Peter Lynch
with John Rothchild

Whatever method you use to pick stocks or stock mutual funds, your ultimate success or failure will depend on your ability to ignore the worries of the world long enough to allow your investments to succeed. It isn't the head but the stomach that determines the fate of the stock-picker.

(Lynch, page 19)

Material quoted within this chapter is extracted from *Beating the Street* by Peter Lynch with John Rothchild, Simon & Schuster, Inc., New York, 1994.

Peter Lynch is a mild-mannered, dedicated workaholic who single-handedly managed the huge and successful Magellan fund for 13 years until his resignation in 1990. If you had invested $1000 in Magellan when he took over in 1977 it would have been worth $28 000 in 1990. Why did he stop? For the best reason in the world – he wanted to spend more time with his family.

> "I've always been skeptical of millionaires who congratulate themselves for walking away from a chance to enrich themselves further. Turning one's back on a fat future paycheck is a luxury few people can afford. But if you're lucky enough to have been rewarded in life to the degree that I have, there comes a point at which you have to decide whether to become a slave to your net worth by devoting the rest of your life to increasing it or to let what you've accumulated begin to serve you."
>
> *(page 8)*

To emphasize the point, he recounts a tale from Tolstoy about a farmer who could have all the land he could circumambulate in a day. After half the day, the farmer has run around enough land to make himself rich, but he keeps going and drops dead of overexertion. "This," writes Lynch, "was the ending I hoped to avoid."

As a fund manager Lynch held a vast portfolio of stocks (over 1400 at any one time) and was constantly changing his positions. On average he turned over the entire portfolio every year.

Clearly, few private investors are able to adopt such a strategy, nor do they need to do so. Lynch says that private investors have their own advantages over the professionals, since they are not obliged by the size of their funds to diversify very much and they are not in competition with one another. If you don't do well in a particular year as a private investor, no-one is ever going to know. There is no spotlight on your performance, no risk to your day-job, and so no pressure on you to take unnecessary risks.

Lynch does believe that you should use company research as much as possible for those stocks you are following; brokers tell him that the majority of their clients fail to take advantage of the data that is on offer.

Most investment books make the point that regular purchases of stocks are advantageous. Lynch puts an interest spin on this:

- if you had invested $1000 in the S & P 500 on January 31, 1940 (this is hypothetical, since there were no index funds then), in 1992 it would be worth over $333 000;
- if you had put a further $1000 into your investment each year over the same period, it would have grown to over $3.5 million;
- best of all, if you had added $1000 to your fund on each of the 31 occasions during those 52 years when the market dropped by 10 percent or more, your money ($83 000 in contributions) would be worth $6 295 000.

Let's consider the implications for a moment: 52 years is likely to be the largest part of your adult life. To invest for that long, you would probably have started in your twenties and continued into old age, long after retirement. During this time, you need not have followed the market obsessively or racked your brains to understand every detail of a vast range of stocks. A diversified portfolio of stocks, large and small, which you studied in your spare time, could easily have yielded a similar result to the S & P 500. You need not have worried much about the economy, the future, market timing or anything else. You could have ignored all the pundits who tell you to trade, or to jump in and out of cash. Simply by adopting a rule to invest $1000 extra each time the market dropped, you would have almost doubled your final result. Six million dollars is a large sum to amass in one lifetime; some people might think that it is not enough, but it is certainly more than adequate for most families' needs. And to achieve such a satisfactory result, no genius has been necessary!

Lynch is very clear on these simple truths. He tells you not to be a "weekend worrier." We are bombarded daily by bad news. Doomsayers are on every side, warning of "global warming, global cooling, the evil Soviet empire, the collapse of the evil Soviet empire, recession, inflation, illiteracy, the high cost of health care, fundamentalist Muslims, the budget deficit, the brain drain, tribal warfare, organized crime, disorganized crime, sex scandals, money scandals, sex and money scandals" ... in short, if you read the newspapers and watch TV, you have a lot to worry about each weekend when you're thinking about your stocks.

Each year Lynch attends an expert panel of fund managers organized by *Barron*'s where "weekend worrying" is raised to a fine art – for the benefit of the journalists, the panelists worry about such matters as G7, the dollar, the Iran–Iraq war, foreign investment in the US and so on. They are never unanimous in their views and, despite their professional expertise, their macroeconomic predictions are not much use. Lynch recommends that you pay no attention to such issues and, more especially, that you do not act on such prognoses. Ignoring bad news, he says, is best done by investing to a regular schedule. He points out that the "Even Bigger Picture" is that in the long-term stocks have out performed other investments. Don't worry about market declines – buy some more stock.

Lynch dislikes bonds, pointing out their vulnerability to inflation. He sees their popularity as misguided. Short-term bonds are best, he thinks, because you can roll them over. At Magellan he did not hold cash or bonds, preferring to purchase good quality stocks with low volatility when he wanted to adopt a defensive position.

Much of the book consists of discussions of a wide range of companies and industries. Lynch likes growth companies, but he also likes troubled industries that are going to recover. There is a long and useful examination of savings and loan associations – simple businesses, retailers, Fannie Maes and so on. In short, he likes anything where he can see, on fundamental grounds, that there is a chance of a profit and he doesn't necessarily plan to hold his stocks for the long-term. His only weak spot seems to be in the high technology arena, which he freely admits he does not understand.

While some of the companies he recommends in the book may no longer offer good value, I suspect that many of them still do. As a handbook on how a very, very successful pro goes about his stock picking, this is an extremely useful work – one to buy, not to borrow.

BUFFETT:
THE MAKING OF AN
AMERICAN CAPITALIST

by

Roger Lowenstein

In the annals of investing, Warren Buffett stands alone. Starting from scratch, simply by picking stocks and companies for investment, Buffett amassed one of the epochal fortunes of the twentieth century. Over a period of four decades – more than enough to iron out the effects of fortuitous rolls of the dice – Buffett outperformed the stock market by a stunning margin and without taking undue risks or suffering a single losing year. This is a feat that market savants, Main Street brokers and academic scholars had long proclaimed to be impossible.

(Lowenstein, page 1)

Material quoted within this chapter is extracted from *Buffett: The Making of an American Capitalist* by Roger Lowenstein, Orion Books Ltd, London, 1996. Part of this chapter first appeared in the UK edition of *Taipan* (Fleet Street Publications) and is reproduced here with kind permission of the publisher.

Warren Buffett is a much-hyped phenomenon and Buffett literature grows apace. I have chosen this book to represent this nerd-made-good (who did so long before Bill Gates's success with Microsoft established the image of the nerdy tycoon in the public imagination) because it is a thorough and balanced biography of an extraordinarily successful investor.

For those who still haven't heard of him, Buffett (pronounced "*Buff*ett") is an investor/fund manager who has amassed a personal fortune of at least $10 billion, working from his home town of Omaha, Nebraska. A pupil of Benjamin Graham (*see* pages 125–132), he has achieved this outstanding result without, it would seem, ever resorting to the kind of chicanery generally expected from moguls. He appears to be a genuine exception to the adage that "behind every great fortune there lies a great crime."

This makes Buffett of special interest to private investors since his methods are possible for the little guy to study and imitate. It is not possible to do this with the methods of a trader such as George Soros because one does not have access to his resources. Buffett, on the other hand, has become rich by using his head and very little else. Private investors hope to do the same.

The biography makes it clear that Buffett has paid a price for his success. He is so concentrated on his work that he does not enjoy his money – Lowenstein calls him "stunted" – nor does he seem to have any interests outside a remarkably narrow field.

There is something slightly tragic about the story of his early life. We are given a picture of an awkward, bespectacled bookworm, highly intelligent, who thought of almost nothing but making money from an early age and who saw everything in terms of numbers. Existential questions were dealt with, for example, by comparing the life spans of the patriarchs of various religions to see which ones lived the longest – and hence which religion might promote the greatest longevity in its adherents.

Buffett's father Howard was a stockbroker turned congressman of extreme rightwing views. His mother is portrayed as a model wife, except for unpredictable outbursts of rage against the children which led the young Warren to spend a good deal of time in other people's homes. In his early teens, his life is pure Horatio Alger. Moving with his family to Washington DC, he developed a series of businesses, starting with a paper route, which he grew by applying standard business methods: improving efficiency, keeping good customer records and analyzing them, increasing the number of product lines and so on. The paper route generated $1200 dollars with which he bought, at the age of 14, 40 acres of Nebraskan agricultural land which he rented to a farmer. A mechanically minded friend could repair pinball machines, so they started a company which had, within a month, three machines in different barber shops. Ever-cautious, Buffett carefully chose out-of-the-way locations for the machines to avoid the attention of gangsters.

Warren and his father were close, and although the son did

not inherit the congressman's isolationist views (Howard voted against the introduction of the Bretton Woods monetary system, postwar aid to Britain and grain exports to Europe) he does seem to have acquired his father's Presbyterian highmindedness about business ethics. They were close, and Warren did not demur when his father insisted that he sell the pin-ball business for $1200 when Warren, at 17, was accepted for the Wharton School of Finance.

Wharton had little to offer Buffett in terms of education – it's suggested that he knew more than his teachers – but it did give him confidence and established a number of friendships which were significant in later life. By 1950, at the age of 19, Buffett had amassed $9800 in cash (he still had the farmland), and this money, Lowenstein tells us, is the source of every dollar Buffett has subsequently earned.

Buffett was turned down by Harvard Business School, which was a shock, and eventually went to Columbia. It was here that he studied under Benjamin Graham, becoming, we are told, Graham's star pupil and acquiring the techniques and methodologies of company analysis – how to read financial statements, how to spot frauds and – one of Graham's favorites – how to profit from "cigar butt" companies with lousy financials but with "a couple of useful puffs" left in them.

When Buffett graduated, both his father, Howard, and Graham advised him not make a career in stocks, but Warren sensibly ignored them. He offered to work for Graham's firm for free and was turned down. The young Warren was shocked when he discovered the reason – that Graham preferred to keep openings at his company for Jews who, at that the time, were unable to obtain positions in gentile firms. Instead of searching elsewhere on Wall Street he returned to a sales job at his father's brokerage in Omaha.

Marrying quickly, Buffett started work pushing a stock he had discovered while at Columbia – GEICO. GEICO was an insurance firm whose chairman was Benjamin Graham. Buffett had detected this fact by looking up his mentor in *Who's Who*. Traveling to GEICO's Washington offices on the weekend, he managed to talk his way into the building and a long interview with an executive who, impressed by the eager beaver's knowledge, explained the workings of the company. Buffett became enamored of the company because of its high profit margins – five times higher than other insurers – and its specialization in low risk clients. Wall Street disagreed; the consensus was that GEICO was overpriced. By the time Buffett had started as a stock salesman he had invested $8000 of his savings in GEICO. The share price doubled in the following two years.

Warren was no salesman – a salesman merely takes a commission, and derives no direct benefit from being right about the companies he recommends. He was too absorbed in the search for investment opportunities. However, clients thought he was inexperienced, and frequently bought stocks which he had recommended through their own brokers.

Ever the self-improver, Buffett, undeterred, decided to become an expert on taxation, and took public speaking courses to develop an authoritative bearing, which he then applied by teaching an investment course. He also invested in a Texaco station and real estate, but these did not turn out well.

Finally the much-hoped-for call came: Graham was willing to take Buffett on at his own firm. Turning down the offer of a loan from his father, Warren returned to New York, determined to make a fortune that was both entirely clean – that is, without deception of any kind, even in the grey areas of tax – and entirely his own work.

There is a great power in monomania. People with a single aim generally do make progress. Yet it would be unfair to Buffett to suggest that this lifelong compulsion to seek out good shares by analysis makes him somehow inhuman. He has always been, by all reports, funny, witty and kind. He enjoys what he does. As we will see later, his integrity and folksy wisdom have enabled to him to turn truly dire situations to his advantage. His simple habits – famously, he lives on steak and hamburgers and, until he switched to Coca-Cola, drank nothing but Pepsi – may be odd but they are hardly dour.

In 1956 Graham retired. There was nothing to keep Buffett in New York so he returned to Omaha with an increased capital of $140 000.

Back in Nebraska, Buffett organized an investment fund with seven limited partners drawn from family and friends. A few more followed and at the age of 26 he found himself in control of several hundred thousand dollars.

Fund managers are usually employees. They tend to move from one firm to the next quite rapidly. This does not encourage them to work in the best interests of their shareholders, say critics. Buffett was different. He was determined to be his own man from then on, and to succeed with the funds he was now managing.

In order to make big money you need start with a large fund, so Warren continued to seek more investors. He was asking for tough terms: investors might only contribute or withdraw capital once a year, and he would not disclose where the money was invested – the aim was to reduce outside interference to a bare minimum. His fees would be based on results, and no fee would be payable if the fund did not perform well. Brashly confident and without a track record, he encountered sales resistance. Although people thought he was honest and had ability, they were reluctant to invest with an untried money manager.

In the first year, Buffett's funds beat the Dow Jones Industrial Average by 2 percent. With his wife about to produce their third child, he purchased a relatively modest five-bedroom house in Omaha where he still lives. By the end of the third year, the original partners' capital had doubled. With a track record developing, more investors came aboard.

At this time, Buffett's share purchases were purely Grahamite; he would seek out companies whose share prices were cheap in relation to their financial statements. He committed vast amounts of company information to memory to aid him. The idea behind buying such bargains is that sooner or later the market will value them more highly but, as Buffett was to discover, sometimes this does not happen. In one such case, Sanborn Map, he was frustrated to realize that while the company's directors were content to cut dividends year after year, they had never once considered cutting their own generous fees. In short, he had encountered one of the main obstacles to value investing, which is that directors of a company may not act in the best interests of shareholders; they may prefer, for instance, not to take actions which would increase the profitability or growth of the company.

The solution was to get himself elected to the board, which was possible when his stockholding in a company was significantly high. As a director of Sanborn Map he kept the pressure on until, in 1960, the board agreed to buy out dissatisfied stockholders, giving him a 50 percent profit on his investment.

By 1962 the Buffett partnerships had $7.2 million in capital, of which $1 million was Buffett's own. Most of the money he earned as a manager was profit-related – if his fund performed above a certain level, he received a percentage, which he then, as a matter of principle, plowed back into the fund. There were now 90 investors spread across the country. Buffett decided to merge all the partnerships into one, called it the Buffett Partnership Ltd, raised the minimum investment to $100 000 and moved into an office in a drab high-rise, Kiewit Plaza, on the same street as his home.

That year he bought a small stake in a Massachusetts textile mill, Berkshire Hathaway, into which he eventually reversed his other operations. Increasingly, Buffett was finding his own style of investing. Unlike Benjamin Graham he was actually interested in companies as businesses; he found himself able to invest in their potential as well as their assets.

The first big play of this kind was American Express, at the time of the salad oil scandal. Amex had a million customers holding the American Express card and half a billion dollars' worth of travelers checks in circulation, but few tangible assets. It was certainly not the kind of company Graham would have liked.

However, in 1963 a salad oil fraud left Amex liable for up to $150 million (a warehouse it owned had been tricked into storing containers of sea water). The stock dropped by a sixth and negative rumors ran wild in the market. After some investigation Buffett decided that Amex was a "franchise" company; its brand name and dominant position in its markets gave it something approaching a monopoly. Buffett started to buy Amex stock.

Two years later Buffett began to load up on Disney, seeing that it, too, had a "franchise" in its characters and magnificent back library of movies. Unlike other fund managers he was not diversifying broadly – most of the money was in a handful of stocks and by 1966, ten years after he had started his partnerships, at the age of 35 he was controlling $44 million. His own share of the fund amounted to a little over $6.5 million.

Buffett's investors were thrilled. Each year he would invite them to his house where he charmed them with self-deprecating tales of his activities. The beginnings of the Buffett cult were founded – he was making people rich and they loved him for it.

The 1960s bull market was in full swing, fueled in part by the industrial expansion supporting the war in Vietnam. Stocks were getting too high for Buffett's liking. The great fashion in investment was the "performance" funds which churned their portfolios rapidly to maximize short-term gains. Buffett looked like a stick-in-the-mud with his long-term attitudes.

By October 1967 Warren couldn't take it any more. The market was looking too crazy. He wrote to his partners, in a now-famous bulletin, that:

> "Essentially I am out of step with present conditions ... I will not abandon a previous approach whose logic I understand even though it may mean forgoing large, and apparently easy, profits to embrace an approach which I don't fully understand, have not practiced successfully, and which, possibly, could lead to substantial permanent loss of capital."
>
> *(page 106) (Letter to partners, 9 October 1967)*

For two more years, however, the Buffett Partnership posted record profits. In 1968 it gained 59 per cent and was worth a total of $104 million. The bull market was in its final throes.

Price/earnings ratios were at insanely high levels – IBM was at 39 and Avon at 56 – and in May 1969 Buffett threw in the towel, announcing that he would liquidate the Buffett Partnership and return the money to his investors. He sold everything except Berkshire Hathaway (which by this time owned an insurance company) and Diversified Retailing, a chain of stores.

Many partners accepted stock in these two companies in lieu of cash. Others followed Buffett's advice and invested in a mutual fund, Sequoia, run by a classmate from Columbia, Bill Ruane, or in municipal bonds, which is where Buffett put his own money.

The liquidation of the Buffett Partnership was an extraordinary move. Financial professionals do not like to give their clients their money back, especially when their performance has been excellent. Warren Buffett was different. He felt that he could not sustain his growth rate and, ever mindful of his reputation, was determined to get out of the market.

As it turned out, his timing was good. Later that year the market crashed; by mid-1970 stocks had halved in price across the board. Buffett had been dramatically vindicated.

Buffett was 40 in 1970. For a while he interested himself in good works, such as funding a liberal newspaper and setting up scholarships for black college students. Like many other plutocrats before him, he began to dabble in social reform. Berkshire Hathaway remained his baby and was soon to be the vehicle of his return.

Slowly, over the next few years, Buffett began to buy small companies outright for Berkshire Hathaway, whose original textile business was doomed. Money was cheap to borrow, so he raised $20 million for the company in corporate bonds through Salomon Brothers. He took large positions in advertising agencies, following a long-cherished dream to get into the media business.

In 1973 he started to buy *Washington Post* stock and soon became its largest external stockholder. Once again, he saw it as a "franchise" business. The *Washington Post*'s board was nervous about his attentions at first – the controlling stockholder was Kay Graham, a shy heiress with little business experience. She feared that this obscure Mid-Western figure was some kind of "ultra-rightwing type" who might be opposed to the *Post*'s liberal views. A rather charming miracle occurred; Warren and Kay became close friends. They developed a platonic relationship of great trust in which Warren provided a magnificent business education while Kay brought him into a rarefied social world and gently knocked off his rough edges. Between 1974 and 1985, the period when Buffett was on the board, the *Post*'s stock rose at a compound rate, including dividends, of 37 percent a year. Berkshire Hathaway's investment of $10 million grew to $205 million.

The following year, Buffett ran into trouble with the SEC. For some time he'd been investing on behalf of three companies – his two "babies," Berkshire Hathaway and Diversified Retail, and

Blue Chip Stamps, in which he was the major stockholder. Warren ran Blue Chip in partnership with a childhood friend and long-time business associate, Charlie Munger. Blue Chip had a trading stamps operation in supermarkets which gave it good positive cashflow, providing funds which Warren and Charlie used to invest in other bargains. Although Buffett wished to be scrupulously fair to all three companies he acted for, each firm had a different set of stockholders and conflict of interest was inevitable.

One of the Blue Chip investments was Wesco Financial which owned a savings and loan. Blue Chip only had $2 million in it but when, in 1973, Wesco had announced a merger, Buffett and Munger were galvanized into action – they saw the merger as a rotten deal for Wesco. In their attempts to prevent the merger they wound up bidding for Wesco, increasing Blue Chip's holding to 24.9 percent. The bid came to nothing, but Blue Chip was now Wesco's biggest stockholder.

These maneuvers attracted the attention of the SEC. In December 1974 it opened a formal investigation of Buffett. Other men might have collapsed under the strain or have done something foolish, but Buffett played it by the book. To rebut allegations that he had manipulated Wesco's stock price he patiently explained his actions, providing thousands of documents for examination.

The inquiry took two years. Slowly the SEC began to realize that Buffett was not a crook and settled in 1976 for minor penalties.

Once the nightmare was over Buffett simplified his operations by consolidating Wesco within Blue Chip and merging Diversified Retailing with Berkshire Hathaway. Berkshire Hathaway was now the parent company of all Buffett's holdings.

By the mid-1970s Buffett was plainly a significant force in the investment world. The enormous sums he deployed meant that he was now playing a game outside the capacity of most private investors. The book continues his story up to 1994, becoming a fascinating tale of big business but of less direct relevance to those of us who are not CEOs of listed companies.

There are two episodes, however, that are worth examining briefly:

- GEICO
- Salomon Brothers

GEICO

Buffett sold his GEICO stock in 1969 when he pulled out of the bull market and liquidated the Buffett Partnership. In 1974 the company was on the verge of bankruptcy and in deep regulatory trouble. After long discussions with the new CEO, Buffett invested and the company gradually turned around following a successful $76 million offering underwritten by Salomon Brothers. The investment has been massively successful over the years and GEICO now forms a significant part of Berkshire Hathaway's ability to generate cash for new acquisitions.

Salomon Brothers

The story of Salomon Brothers, a bond trading and company underwriting firm, in the 1980s is well told in Michael Lewis's *Liar's Poker* (*see* pages 141–148). Buffett became increasingly close to its boss, John Gutfreund, and by the late 1980s was receiving calls from him several times a week. In 1987, when Salomon was in trouble, Buffett agreed to support it by an investment of $700 million in convertible bonds, which are safer than equities. He and Charlie Munger were given seats on the board. Buffett rarely intervenes in the management of the companies in which he has an interest, but he promptly voted against the other directors when they wanted to increase the already absurdly generous bonuses. He was overruled.

When the news broke in 1989 that a greedy trader had made fraudulent bids for new Treasury issues and that Gutfreund had hushed the matter up, Salomon Brothers collapsed into chaos. Buffett's investment was, he believed, safe even if the company were liquidated, but when Gutfreund asked him to take over as CEO he couldn't resist the challenge.

Despite warnings that his reputation could be ruined if he were associated with a scandal of this magnitude, Buffett took over, rapidly instituting changes and, once again, co-operating fully with the SEC investigation. After nine months of bitter struggle to rescue the firm – which he succeeded in doing – Buffett stepped down as chairman, retaining his investment and handing over the helm to a "colorless administrator." The book tells us that, as of 1994, the jury is still out on whether this was the right decision.

How to invest in Buffett

While we may not all be able to imitate Buffett's investment success, it is still possible to participate in his operations by investing in Berkshire Hathaway. In this section we'll look at some reasons for doing so.

First, a few facts:

- Warren Buffett is one of the richest men in the world, with a net worth of well over 10 billion dollars.

- He controls, manages and is the part-owner of Berkshire Hathaway Inc., which he bought in 1965. Under his leadership Berkshire Hathaway has become an enormous investment company which owns and operates hugely successful businesses as well as being a major shareholder in such blue chips as Coca-Cola and American Express.

- Buffett began his career with $9800 in 1950; he'd accumulated this cash during his teens by running newspaper routes and some pinball machines in barber shops. This $9800 is the source of every penny he has subsequently earned in the investment business.

- Over the last 33 years (since Buffett took control of the company) the per share book value of Berkshire Hathaway has grown by 24.1 percent each year (annually compounded).

- In 1997 the per share book value grew by 34.1 percent.

The honest billionaire

So how does he do it? First of all, he is the ultimate bean counter who does nothing but follow his investments. He stays most of the time in his home town of Omaha, Nebraska, lives on soda pop and cheeseburgers and doesn't spend much money on fripperies. Okay, he finally bought a company jet, but only with much embarrassment and apologies. The man can do complex calculations rapidly in his head – he doesn't need advisers or computers to do his sums for him.

Second, he is honest. Buffett is just one of those rare people who tries to tell the truth all the time. He has shown himself to be more than just a "miserable accumulator" (a phrase used by his long-time business partner, Charlie Munger) – he genuinely sees his tens of thousands of shareholders as being equal partners in Berkshire Hathaway, and doesn't exploit his position to enrich himself at the expense of the other shareholders. He can be tough – he'll close down a company and put the employees out of work with little more than the legally required severance terms – but he just doesn't cheat or break the law, ever.

Numerous books have been written on Buffett's investment philosophy and methods, which are, frankly, pretty hard to understand when it comes to the details. The main thing you need to know is that he is basically a long-term investor who is very choosy about his stock picks; he looks for companies that are, in his judgement, both excellent businesses and blessed with outstandingly able directors who have integrity. He can't be bothered dealing with crooks – which rules out a large number of public companies right away. He's a good writer, so if you want to know more about how his mind works, read his annual reports – they're on the Internet at:

http://www.berkshirehathaway.com

Try the Class B shares

If he's such a genius, why doesn't everyone just give him their money? One reason is that until 1997, smaller investors simply couldn't – a single share was costing around $40,000. Normally when a company is successful and its shares reach a very high price, there will be a stock split or some other form of issue to make the shares look "cheaper." Buffett resisted the pressures to do this for a number of reasons, the most important being that he doesn't particularly want to attract short-term investors. About 97 percent of his shareholders stay with him, year in and year out, and that's the way he likes it. He also doesn't want to risk getting taken over by a predator.

In May 1997 Buffett took pity on the numerous small investors who just couldn't afford to buy even one share of Berkshire Hathaway, and issued a new class of shares ("B" shares) which cost considerably less. To protect himself from unwelcome investors, he has given the "B" shares fewer voting rights than the main shares, now called the "A" shares.

A Class "B" share has the rights of 1/30th of a Class "A" share, except that it only has 1/200th of the voting rights of a

Class "A" share (rather than 1/30th of the voting rights). Class "A" shares can be converted into 30 Class "B" shares, but Class "B" shares cannot be converted.

If you buy a Class "B" stock, you are entitled to go to the AGM, which is held in May in Omaha, Nebraska, and is, by all accounts, a fascinating and enjoyable event – you may get to meet some of the hundreds of investors who have become millionaires by simply sticking with Buffett for years. As he likes to say, "a full and happy life can still be yours" if you leave calculations to others whom you can trust.

At the time of writing, a Class "A" share costs you $68 000 and a Class "B" share costs you $2270.

The future

Buffett is really serious about investing for the long-term; he believes that it is the "intrinsic value" rather than the market capitalization or the book value of a company that really counts. Like his famous mentor, the share analyst Benjamin Graham, he thinks that the stockmarket eventually "wakes up" to the intrinsic value of a company, but that this can take years. Although he aims to beat the S & P index each year, the really impressive gains come when the businesses that he invests in grow in real terms (that is, when they sell more goods and services, make more profits, acquire more real assets) and the stock market recognizes this.

He reckons that it is much tougher to make money now that Berkshire Hathaway is so large – in the early days, a million dollar gain had an astonishing effect on the company's growth figures, but now a similar gain would barely register.

We'll see. The insurance company, GEICO, which is 100 percent owned by Berkshire Hathaway, has been doing fabulously well. Overall, the net earnings of the insurance segment of the company nearly doubled between 1995 and 1997 – from $496 400 000 to $952 600 000. That's almost a billion dollars in net earnings. One of Buffett's most endearing characteristics is that he likes to be conservative in his forecasts. In the end, if he can't find anywhere good to invest the money his businesses generate, he'll distribute it to the shareholders – we can believe that he'll do this because he did it once before, in the late 1960s.

If you buy BRK.A or BRK.B (the NYSE symbols for the two classes of stock), hold them for the long-term. How long is that? At least until Warren Buffett dies; he's 68 now, but he's the kind of man who will go on working effectively until he drops – like Getty, Hammer and other tycoons who ran their empires well into their nineties. He's done his best to secure the succession so that the company will continue its extraordinary trajectory far into the 21st century, but even geniuses can't control what happens after they die.

COMMON STOCKS
AND UNCOMMON
PROFITS
AND OTHER WRITINGS

by

Philip A. Fisher

In studying the investment record both of myself and others, two matters were significant influences in causing this book to be written. One, which I mention several times elsewhere, is the need for patience if big profits are to be made from investment. Put another way, it is often easier to tell what will happen to the price of a stock than how much time will elapse before it happens. The other is the inherently deceptive nature of the stock market. Doing what everybody else is doing at the moment, and therefore what you have an almost irresistible urge to do, is often the wrong thing to do at all.

(Fisher, page 4)

Material quoted within this chapter is extracted from *Common Stocks and Uncommon Profits and Other Writing*s by Philip A. Fisher, John Wiley & Sons, Inc., New York, 1996.

Philip Fisher has been a money manager for more than half a century, starting out in 1931. His central idea is to identify outstandingly good businesses – which, by definition, are rare – and hold their stock almost indefinitely. Three of his own successes were Texas Instruments (bought in the original private placement and held for decades), Dow Chemicals and Motorola.

Warren Buffett has said that as an investor he is "85 percent Graham and 15 percent Fisher," apparently meaning that a dash of business assessment helps to liven up the plainness of value investment.

Fisher is a prolix writer. He doesn't always say what he means, and when he does he says it several times over. His ideas are not well-organized and he writes at length in generalities that are hard to apply. You can see why he is good at "scuttlebutt" (a word he coined to refer to using the business grapevine to research companies). Scuttlebutt is all about scavenging for information; you don't know what you are going to get or what order you are going to get it in, so you allow the picture to emerge slowly. It's the same with his book, which is a rambling collection of insights, anecdotes, injunctions, half-hearted attempts at structuring ideas. It's a kind of master investor's mandala-in-progress, useful but not easy to read.

The secrets of scuttlebutt

Fisher believes that there are many things you can and should discover about a company which do not appear in the published accounts. The only way to get this information, he says, is to obtain a wide cross-section of opinions from people associated with a company: employees, ex-employees, customers, suppliers, academics, trade association officers, industry observers, salespeople at trade shows and so on. He emphasizes that you must be discreet and promise never to repeat what you are told; in return you will find that people will talk remarkably freely:

> "Go to five companies in an industry, ask each of them intelligent questions about the points of strength and weakness of the other four, and nine times out of ten a surprisingly detailed and accurate picture of all five will emerge."

> *(page 17)*

Can anyone use scuttlebutt? Plainly not – you have to be willing to spend a great amount of time and effort on it. But If you have the right turn of mind, and you are looking for very, very special companies which will grow strongly for many decades, then investing time in scuttlebutt makes sense.

Fisher's 15 stock-picking criteria

According to Fisher, good businesses can be identified by their performance against certain criteria. Here is a brief summary of Fisher's "points system" that he outlines in *Common Stocks and Uncommon Profits*; ideally, an outstanding company will yield positive answers to almost all the questions:

1. *Does the company currently have the potential of several years'*

sales growth? Fisher divides these between the "fortunate and able," that are well-managed but also benefit from an unforeseeable improvement in their businesses, and the "fortunate because they are able," that benefit from new markets stimulated by innovative products. He gives several examples of companies that have enjoyed extraordinary growth, including Motorola, Alcoa and Du Pont.

2. *Is the company likely to produce new products and processes in the future?* Many products have a short life at high profits; companies need to keep introducing new ones to maintain their margins over many years.

3. *Is the R&D department effective, given the company's size?* Clearly, larger companies can afford larger R & D budgets. Fisher says that the level of cost/benefit in R & D spend varies widely between companies. He recommends using "scuttlebutt" to augment the rough figures obtainable from published accounts.

4. *Does the company have an above-average sales organization?* A strong "sales arm" is the best guarantee that profits will grow as planned.

5. *Does the company have a worthwhile profit margin?* Fisher does not specify what he thinks high and low profit margins are, but seems to assess them against margins prevailing in an industry or generally. He says that "the greatest long-range investment profits are never obtained in marginal companies" (i.e., low-profit companies). The only exception is

where a company spends part of its profits on extra sales promotion or research in order to speed growth – the effectiveness of this must be assessed carefully, but if it is real, the company may achieve excellent growth acceleration.

6. *What is the company doing to maintain or improve profit margins?* Direct questioning of company personnel should reveal this – it is one of the topics which senior executives are generally willing to talk about in detail.

7. *Does the company have outstanding labor and personnel relations?* Employers who are good to their staff enjoy loyalty and the pick of the best new applicants. Avoid companies where the management have a negative or exploitative attitude towards the workforce.

8. *Does the company have outstanding executive relations?* The same applies to the management. Fisher says you can get a sense of this by talking to executives at several different levels of seniority within the firm.

9. *Does the company have depth to its management?* Are executives given their heads and allowed to make their own decisions? Are they being developed for greater responsibility? Fisher thinks they should be.

10. *How good are the company's cost analysis and accounting controls?* This is hard to appraise – "only in instances of extreme inefficiency" will an outsider be likely to get a clear picture.

11. *Are there other aspects of the business ... which will give the investor important clues as to how outstanding the company may*

be in relation to its competition? For instance, does a retail company handle its real estate leases well? Use scuttlebutt.

12. *Is the company short-termist or long-termist?* Fisher prefers companies that seek to build their profits over the long-term rather than attempting to maximize them in the short-term.

13. *Will there be equity financing in the near future that will damage the stockholders' interests?* Fisher is obscure on this point – he does suggest, though, that when you calculate the number of shares outstanding, you assume that all senior convertible issues have been converted to shares and that all warrants and options have been exercised.

14. *Do managers talk freely to investors when all is well but clam up when there is trouble?* Avoid companies that try to hide bad news.

15. *Does the management have integrity?* Managers have more control over their company than do the stockholders. They can pay themselves too much, have snug arrangements to sell the company goods and services provided by their own private firms, abuse their power to issue stock options and perpetrate numerous other scams which in effect, steal profits from the stockholders. Use scuttlebutt to assess whether or not the managers have real integrity.

Fisher's 10 "don'ts"

Fisher also reminds us of a number of common errors that investors make when they are searching for growth stocks. In the present author's opinion, they are all very sound warnings, except for point 9, which is about timing and is perhaps too difficult for outsiders to practice successfully:

1. *Don't buy in to promotional companies.* Fisher points out that the chances of selecting a successful company which is already established (i.e., that it has had at least three years' trading and one year of operating profits) is much higher than if it is a start-up. He thinks start-up financing should be left to specialists.

2. *Don't ignore a good stock just because it is traded "over the counter."* After discussing the changing face of the markets during the century, and the problems of marketability of stocks, Fisher concludes that over the counter stocks with two or more market-making brokers will provide sufficient marketability for the smaller investor – you can sell shares.

3. *Don't buy a stock just because you like the "tone" of the annual report.* It is hard to believe that some people invest in shares because of the public relations efforts in the annual report, but professional advisers assure us that they do. This rule is simply pointing out that companies wish to look their best in public and that you cannot expect to get the whole story from an annual report.

4. *Don't assume that a high price at which a stock may be selling in relation to earnings is necessarily an indication that further growth in those earnings has largely been already discounted in the price.* In other words, companies with high price/earnings

ratios may continue to enjoy growth in earnings which will lead to eventual price rises – so don't rule them out as investments.

5. *Don't quibble over eighths and quarters.* Don't get hung up on the exact price when buying or selling stocks.

6. *Don't overstress diversification.* Fisher uses that metaphor of an infantryman stacking rifles. He can get a firmer stack by balancing five rifles together rather than two, but he can't get a firmer stack by using 50 rifles instead of five. Diversification into between five and ten stocks is all that is necessary.

7. *Don't be afraid to buy on a war scare.* Fisher says that American markets have always plunged when either a major war has broken out or American forces have been fighting, with the single exception of the outbreak of World War II when there was a short-lived rally. "War is always bearish on money" – spare cash should go into stocks at this time.

8. *Don't forget your Gilbert and Sullivan.* Fisher applies the lines from a Gilbert and Sullivan song that "flowers that bloom in the spring, tra-la ... have nothing to do with the case" to historical price movements and historical per-share earnings. He points out that growth stocks may change rapidly and that such statistics will give no hint of such changes before they occur.

9. *Don't fail to consider time as well as price in buying a true growth stock.* If you find a great growth stock which meets all

Fisher's criteria, its price may be fluctuating substantially. If you believe that the stock will go up to 75 in five years' time, do you buy at the current price, say 32, or hope that the price will dip to 20, which you regard as its "true value?" Fisher says that by studying the industry you may be able to divine a point in the development of similar companies when the price jumps – say, just before a plant goes into production. He suggests that you pick a fixed date on which to buy, based on this information. This does not sound like a wise move for non-professionals.

10. *Don't follow the crowd.* We are constantly being told not to do this – and we could be forgiven for wondering whether we aren't just going to follow the crowd of non-crowd followers. Fisher's point is essentially that the financial community is subject to moods which last several years – in a good mood, the markets will overvalue certain things, such as stocks in general, a particular industry or a particular set of measures, while at other times they will undervalue them. Institutional investors help to create fads and, because of the size of their funds, help to destroy them when they change their minds. Private investors should ignore the market's "mood."

Great investors like Warren Buffett sing Philip Fisher's praises, and at least one generation of stock market professionals has adopted his insights as received wisdom, but it is not necessarily easy to find great growth stocks by any mechanical application of his criteria. Much more important, I suspect, is the ability to use your judgement – if you have the experience, it is possible to get a "feel" for a young company's prospects. You need to find only two or three really great growth stocks in a lifetime to obtain extraordinary returns. Read Fisher to see how a man with that magic touch tried, somewhat unsuccessfully, to explain how he did it.

CONFUSION DE CONFUSIONES

by

Joseph Penso de la Vega

A high price of shares causes concern to many who are not accustomed to it. But reasonable men need not be disturbed about the matter, since every day the position of the [East India] Company becomes more splendid, the state wealthier, and the revenue from investments at fixed interest becomes less, in as much as it is difficult to find ways of investing money.

(Fridson, ed., page 164)

Material quoted within this chapter is extracted from *Extraordinary Popular Delusions and the Madness of Crowds and Confusión de Confusiones*, edited by Martin S. Fridson, John Wiley & Sons, Inc., New York, 1996.

Unlike *Extraordinary Popular Delusions and the Madness of Crowds* (pages 89–97), *Confusión de Confusiones* is an authentic primary historical source. Issued in 1688 by Joseph de la Vega, a Portuguese Jew, and written in Spanish, it is a series of dialogues explaining the operation of the Amsterdam stock exchange of his time. Its main value to modern investors is that it vividly demonstrates that there is nothing new about the intricate dealings of market players – the speculators of 17th-century Amsterdam would have soon adapted themselves to today's Wall Street.

In the book, a Philosopher and a Merchant interrogate a Shareholder about the workings of the bourse, which the Shareholder says is:

> " ... this enigmatic business which is at once the fairest and most deceitful in Europe, the noblest and most infamous in the world, the finest and most vulgar on earth. It is the quintessence of academic learning and a paragon of fraudulence; it is a touchstone for the intelligent and a tombstone for the audacious, a treasury of usefulness and a source of disaster, and finally a counterpart of Sisyphus who never rests as also of Ixion, who is chained to a wheel that turns perpetually."

(page 147)

Although speculation in commodities had existed for centuries, dealing in stocks was something relatively new. At Amsterdam in the 1680s there was only one principal stock, the Dutch East India Company, established in 1602, and a lesser one, the Dutch West

India Company. East India Company stock had originally been issued at 3000 guilders per share, but in 1688 it was trading at about 17 000 guilders. Like the high-priced Berkshire Hathaway "A" stock of today (some $70,000 per share at the time of writing), the high price of the stock made it unaffordable for smaller investors. This, says Professor Hermann Kellenbenz in his 1957 introduction, was possibly the cause of the emergence of many devices for speculating in the stock without *bona fide* dealing. Kellenbenz explains that there were five main types of transaction:

- sales of stock for cash;
- sales of stock where up to 80 percent of the price was borrowed;
- forward contracts for purchase of the stock at a specified future date. Most of these deals were short sales, which were illegal, but were conducted by using loopholes in the law;
- options – puts, calls and possibly straddles;
- trading in "ducaton" shares, which were unofficial shares with a nominal value of 10 percent of the real stock.

De la Vega says that there are three types of men in the market, the "princes of business," the merchants and the speculators. The "princes" receive their dividends and hold on to their stock indefinitely. The merchants buy and sell stock in the hope of capital gains at relatively low risk and the lowest class, the speculators, take crazy risks and try to manipulate the market. The great players of today's markets, the financial institutions, were then unknown.

Although he writes in a florid, overblown style, as can be seen from the extract on page 85, de la Vega clearly knew the operations of the market well, and describes them clearly. Kellenbenz thinks he is shaky on the law, but the author is sharp enough on the actual matter of profit and loss. Much of what de la Vega regards as chicanery – in particular the activities of brokers and market makers – is institutionalized today, but in general his analysis seems sophisticated. He describes a dynamic system of contending forces, ever vulnerable to news from the outside (such as war scares), perpetually attempting to make the market go their way but never succeeding for very long; he asserts that it is possible to make a good and honest living from the market if you are sensible. To emphasize his point, he has the Merchant conclude at the end of the book that :

> "... I esteem business but hate gambling ... It is possible that I shall become a holder of shares and shall deal in an honest way, but I am very sure that I shall never become a speculator ..."
>
> *(page 211)*

while the Philosopher decides that he prefers philosophy to wealth-gathering.

So is it all just ancient history, irrelevant to our brave new world? It's easy to think of our ancestors as being brutal and deluded; but here in these pages is evidence, if any were needed, that they were just as smart as we are and, in many ways, considerably more realistic.

EXTRAORDINARY POPULAR DELUSIONS AND THE MADNESS OF CROWDS

by

Charles Mackay

But the most absurd and preposterous of all, and which shewed [showed] more completely than any other, the utter madness of the people, was one started by an unknown adventurer, entitled "A company for carrying on an undertaking of great advantage, but nobody to know what it is."

(Fridson, ed., page 78)

Material quoted within this chapter is extracted from *Extraordinary Popular Delusions and the Madness of Crowds and Confusión de Confusiones*, edited by Martin S. Fridson, John Wiley & Sons, Inc., New York, 1996.

First published in 1846 as *Memoirs of Extraordinary Popular Delusions*, this book is widely regarded as being one of the great investment classics. Written by a Scottish journalist, it is in fact a collection of stories, retold from other sources, of examples of mass movements and crazes. Only part deals with financial speculations – the rest delves into such matters as catchphrases in the streets of London and medieval witch hunting, which, although they are "crowd madness," are not relevant to investment.

Like many other books with wonderfully intriguing titles, it fails to deliver on its promise. *Extraordinary Popular Delusions and the Madness of Crowds* is an inadequate book, carelessly compiled and full of inaccuracies. This is a shame, since its topic is fascinating. Mass hysteria is real. We know well that it is possible to influence large groups of people through organized manipulation and also that crazes often occur spontaneously when conditions are right. But if you want a scientific approach to these matters, this is not the book to read.

What *Delusions* does offer the investor is a précis of three speculative booms and busts, the Mississippi Scheme and the South Sea Bubble of the early 18th century and the Dutch tulip craze of 1634–7 (two of these are summarized below). It is very far from being the last word on these events, but it serves as a basic introduction. It is important that investors should contemplate boom/busts of the past if they want to survive them in the future, so think of this book as a kind of light inoculation against going crazy at a bull top.

The Dutch tulip mania

In the middle of the 1500s the tulip was first introduced into Europe from Turkey, gradually becoming highly prized as an exotic plant for the gardens of the wealthy. By the 1630s the tulip trade had mushroomed, and Holland experienced a wild boom in prices. A bulb of the "Admiral Liefkin" variety was worth 4400 florins, while an "Admiral Van Der Eyck" was worth 1260 florins – at a time when a new carriage with a pair of horses and harnesses was worth about 4600 florins. Mackay tells several stories of individuals who unwittingly ate or cut tulip bulbs, only to be thrown into prison until they could pay the vast debts incurred by the damage they'd caused. Bulbs were traded in stock exchanges across Holland, and the entire population of the country became involved in the speculation.

Here's how Mackay describes the beginning of the bust:

> "At last, however, the more prudent began to see that this folly could not last for ever. Rich people no longer bought the flowers to keep them in their gardens, but to sell them again at cent per cent profit. It was seen that somebody must lose fearfully in the end. As this conviction spread, prices fell, and never rose again."
>
> *(page 119)*

Defaults began on a grand scale. Lawsuits multiplied like fungus but the courts threw most of the cases out, saying that the tulip speculation amounted to gambling and gambling debts were not legally enforceable.

The introduction to the 1996 edition, published by John Wiley & Sons, tells us that Peter M. Garber, of Brown University, has shown that Mackay "sloppily assembled his history from secondhand sources" and argues that there were equally large price swings for rare bulbs both earlier and later than the 1634–7 mania; the wild speculation of that period was centered on the common varieties of tulip rather than the rare ones. "Tulipmania," however, has passed into market folklore as the ultimate in lunatic bubbles, largely because of Mackay's book.

John Law and the Mississippi Scheme

John Law was a Scottish banker, born in 1671, who killed a man in a duel in England and had to flee the country. An advertisement offering a reward for his capture describes him as:

"Captain John Law, a Scotchman, aged twenty six; a very tall, black, lean man; well-shaped, above six feet high, with large pock-holes in his face; big-nosed and speaking broad and loud."

(page 25)

Law traveled in continental Europe for three years before returning to Scotland where he published a pamphlet entitled *Proposals and Reasons for Constituting a Council of Trade*. Law was something of a financial genius, and when his proposals for a reformed national bank were dropped, Law returned to Europe to wander and gamble. He befriended a number of French aristocrats at the gambling tables and was soon attempting to sell his idea for a "land-bank," which backed its currency with the nation's real estate, to the government of France.

At the time, France was in economic turmoil. It had, says Mackay, a national debt of some 3000 million livres and could not meet the interest payable. Various efforts, such as debasing the coinage and a savage program of fines and expropriations, were unsuccessful in stabilizing the situation. Law got himself presented at court and proposed to the regent that a national bank should be set up to manage the revenues of the crown. In 1716 he was authorized to open a private bank, Law and Company, which could issue notes that were acceptable as payment for taxes and had a fixed capital of 6 million livres.

Law made his notes exchangeable for any coins then current. This was a masterstroke, because while the coinage was being debased, Law's notes held good. Within a year they were trading at a 15 percent premium to their face value and his fame was assured. Mackay asserts that his bank restored business confidence and helped to revive trade.

Now that he had the regent eating out of his hand, Law asked him for permission to set up a company which would have exclusive rights to trade on the Mississippi river and the vast French province in North America of Louisiana (much larger than today's state). He received his permission in 1717.

Law had become a favorite of the court and of the people. His bank was given the right of monopoly to the tobacco trade and gold and silver refining and then was made the Royal Bank of

France. Once it was a public institution, it issued 1000 million livres at, says Mackay, the behest of the regent. This money was not backed up by assets. A crisis erupted when the parliament defied the regent and tried to oust Law: but this attempt failed when the regent had the president and two counselors arrested.

In 1719 the Mississippi Company was given a monopoly right to trade in the East Indies, China, the South Seas and all the possessions of the French East India Company. Law changed the name to the Company of the Indies and issued more shares, guaranteeing a 40 percent annual dividend. The shares could be paid for with the old *billets d'état* which were trading at a discount to their nominal value.

The issue was wildly oversubscribed by the public and with the price of the old shares rocketing, Law decided to issue another 300 000 shares at 5000 livres each. A semi-permanent fair sprang up in Paris, attracting speculators from all classes who were desperate to obtain Law's shares.

The shares sometimes rose "10 or 20 percent" in a few hours and many people were enriched. Prices in Parisian stores shot up and the city experienced a boom. Law had become the most important man in the kingdom. He bought fine estates and converted to Roman Catholicism in return for being made comptroller-general of the country's finances.

The bubble continued until 1720. An aristocratic enemy attempted to cause a run on the bank by converting his notes to gold and silver, but failed. Sensing trouble ahead, people started to whisk their stores of precious metal abroad, while the government issued proclamations devaluing the coinage further and Law began to restrict the amount of specie that could be exchanged for notes.

In a crazy move, the government forbade individuals from owning more than 500 livres of coins and from hoarding jewelry and precious metals. The Mississippi Company's stock began to fall – the company had not yet produced any wealth from its trading monopolies.

In May, the government announced that the notes of Law's bank and the shares of the Company of the Indies would be devalued gradually to 50 percent of their nominal value by the end of the year. The parliament objected and the regent retracted the edict. The bank stopped paying specie for notes altogether and Law was dismissed and made the scapegoat.

The government then abolished the ban on holding coins and printed new notes, withdrawing the old ones. Riotous scenes occurred as people swarmed to the bank to change their money. By October it was announced that Mississippi Company notes in large denominations would be worthless in a month's time, and the company was stripped of its monopolies.

Not long afterwards, the regent gave Law permission to leave the country. Once he'd gone, his lands were seized and the regent continued to lay the blame on Law for issuing too many bank notes.

In 1729, Law died in Venice a poor man. France stumbled on

towards its Revolution. Mackay portrays John Law as honest, a victim of a corrupt government. This rings true – there are very good reasons why the central banks of today must behave as independently as they do, inviting accusations of treason and incompetence. Law's early attempt at creating one shows what happens when a banker becomes a puppet of the politicians.

One of the most interesting aspects of the 18th-century bubbles is the close involvement of the State. Indeed, I suspect that no bubble can ever form without the catalyst of government action. Painful memories of what has gone before encourage people to grab what they can while it lasts; everyone knows, consciously or unconsciously, that it has to end sometime but no-one knows when. This is the essence of the phenomenon. It's a test of character, not of cunning, since the people who are left standing after the crash will have had to have reined in their greed and endured the unpleasant experience of seeing everyone else making fortunes while they themselves remained idle. For most of us, resisting peer pressure is the most difficult challenge we can ever face.

45 YEARS IN
WALL STREET

by

W. D. Gann

Buy when the market is making higher Tops and higher Bottoms which shows that the main trend is up. Sell when the market is making lower Tops and lower Bottoms which indicates the main trend is down. Time periods are always important. Check the Time period from previous Top to Top and from previous Bottom to Bottom. Also check the Time required for the market to move up from extreme low to extreme high and the Time required for prices to move down from extreme high to extreme low.

(Gann, page 12)

Material quoted within this chapter is extracted from *45 Years in Wall Street* by W.D. Gann, Lambert Gann Publishing Co., Inc., Pomeroy, WA, 1976.

William Gann is like a religion – either you believe in him or you don't. Although he is one of the key figures in the pantheon of technical analysts, his writings make the other pundits seem positively lucid.

For half a century Gann was in and around Wall Street as a commentator and speculator. Not much is known for certain about his actual investment results, but from the large number of books, pamphlets and correspondence courses he wrote and published over the years, it would appear that he was unable to support himself solely from his market operations.

I feel sorry for William Gann. There are stories that he was a practicing occultist; not the amusing kind who capers around naked in the woods, but the anal-retentive kind who thinks you can predict the future by poring over patterns – in his case, the patterns of stock price movements. To Gann, this was "studying." He seems to have disguised this interest, if the stories are true, in his public writings but it is plain that he was enamored of the occult idea that there are universal repeating patterns in nature.

There are, of course, many widely occurring patterns in nature, but there is also randomness. Read *A Random Walk Down Wall Street* (pages 175–183) for a clear discussion of this extraordinary phenomenon of patternlessness.

In the world according to Gann, however, the world is nothing but patterns which replicate one another on every scale – hence if you know the "secret" of the patterns, you can predict just about anything. He is most famous for his "angles" (formed by trend lines against the axes of charts) and also of certain numerical sequences, which he discusses in this book. Here's a sample:

> "One of the greatest discoveries I ever made was how to figure the percentage of high and low prices on the averages and individual stocks. The percentage of extreme high and low levels indicate future resistance levels ... The most important resistance level is 50 percent on the lowest selling price on the averages or individual stocks ..."

(page 30)

Gann's writing is often described as obscure – perhaps you can see why. What he appears to be saying here is that if you add 50 percent to a historically low price – he doesn't say how he identifies this – then you have a number at which you can anticipate a "resistance level" in the future, that is, a high point which the stock price will reach and bounce back from, perhaps several times, before eventually breaking through it or dropping more permanently.

If, say, the low price for a given stock is 60 then you can expect a resistance level at 90 in the future and a weaker one (using the 100 percent rule) at 120.

Traders still use Gann, just as they use Fibonacci numbers, the Elliott Wave and a host of other systems to try to make sense of what they do. You can still take Gann courses and attend lectures by Gann gurus. Nobody, however, seems to have succeeded in codifying his theories.

A quantity of trading rules are given in *45 Years in Wall Street*, many of which appear to make sense and are still used today. For example:

- Divide your trading capital into 10 equal parts and don't use more than one part (i.e., 10 percent of the total) on any one trade.
- Use stop loss orders of between 3 and 5 points below the purchase price.
- Diversify into four or five stocks.
- Don't average down by buying more of a losing stock.

Some of the rules seem to contradict others, such as "When in doubt, get out" versus "Don't close your trades without a good reason."

This may be unfair to Gann, but the present writer is of the John Train school of thought, which simply asks "Why aren't technical analysts rich? Why aren't great investors like Buffett and Soros technical analysts?" The response of Gannites to such questions seem to be deliberate mystification – namely that it takes "years of study" to understand Gann and that he is "profound." Let's see the evidence – it isn't in his books, which are slight, badly written and more than a little eccentric.

Nevertheless, Gann is taken so seriously by a die-hard minority of investors, particularly traders, that students of the market need to know something about him, which is why I have included *45 Years in Wall Street* among the 25 classics. For a comprehensive and less obscure introduction to the black art of technical analysis, read *Technical Analysis of Stock Trends* by Edwards and McGee (*see* pages 203–208).

THE
GREAT CRASH 1929

by

J. K. Galbraith

The pages that follow tell of the greatest cycle of specula
tive boom and collapse in modern times – since, in fact, the
South Sea Bubble. There is merit in keeping alive the
memory of those days. For it is neither public regulation
nor the improving moral tone of corporate promoters, brokers, customer's men, market operators, bankers and
mutual fund managers which prevents these recurrent
outbreaks and their aftermath. It is the recollection of
how, on some past occasion, illusion replaced reality and
people got rimmed.

(Galbraith, page 9)

Material quoted within this chapter is extracted from *The Great Crash 1929*
by J. K. Galbraith, Penguin, London, 1992.

Much has been written about the Wall Street Crash, but little by so towering a figure as John Kenneth Galbraith, Paul M. Warburg Professor of Economics *emeritus* at Harvard University.

Born in 1908, Galbraith has the advantage of having been alive at the time of the crash, although his own *floreat* did not begin until World War II when, in his early thirties, he was put in charge of price controls at the American Office of Price Administration – a position he recently described as being the most important job he ever held.

Galbraith is an economist of liberal tendencies; closely identified with the Kennedy administration and the Democratic party in general, he has long been an advocate of what might be called the "good husbandry" approach to economics, as opposed to the pursuit of growth at any cost. As such, his ideas are back in fashion.

The Great Crash 1929 is a short history of the US stock market bubble of the 1920s, written in the 1950s. The author has been at pains to avoid presenting the reader with much heavyweight economic analysis, but while purists may argue that more recent developments in economics shed new light on the "causes" of the crash and the Great Depression that followed, the book provides investors with a good idea of the course of events. It is strangely reassuring to find politicians, bankers and market commentators reacting in similar ways in the 1920s as they have during more recent financial crises; investors –

always assaulted by expert pronouncements – can comfort themselves with the thought that no-one is ever completely right about the market.

The 1929 crash has such a legendary status that enterprising investors might begin to feel that they themselves might not have been fooled by the bonanza – that when stocks became ridiculously overvalued, they would have pulled out of the market completely. Galbraith shows how even the small minority who were alarmed at the scale of the boom were wrong in their prognostications.

Poor's *Weekly Business and Investment Letter*, for instance, spoke of the "great common stock delusion" in the autumn of 1928 and the *Commercial and Financial Chronicle* went out of its way to feature any bad news that became available. The *New York Times* continuously argued that stock prices had to crash and on several occasions announced that the crash had actually occurred – prematurely as it turned out. There were breaks in the market in June and December of 1928 and in February and March of 1929, but, unfortunately for the skeptics, stock prices resumed their ascent.

Galbraith tells us that by the summer of 1929 news of the stockmarket had come to dominate popular culture – and that even intellectuals who at other times might have been immersed in *recherché* subjects like Proust and psychoanalysis were now as mesmerized by stocks as everyone else. He describes various attempts, both successful and unsuccessful, to manipulate the market during this period, but does not view such chicanery as being a major factor in the crash that eventually came.

During the boom, says the author, the public's attitude towards insider trading was not one of outrage at the rule-breaking, but rather that they wished they could have a piece of the action too. In 1929 stockbrokers' offices were packed all day with customers who preferred to watch the board where price changes were listed than to attend to their own work.

In early September the market began to slip. No-one was particularly worried. A chartist named Roger Babson was blamed for the break – he'd predicted, on 5 September, that "… factories will shut down … men will be thrown out of work … the vicious circle will then get in full swing and the result will be a serious business depression." Brokers and the press denounced him as a false prophet.

Galbraith goes on to say that the accepted view of the crash was that by 1929 the US economy was heading for trouble; industrial production, the transportation of goods and house building were all declining. In his own opinion, however, the decline was not great and it was reasonable to assume, prior to the market crash, that the economic decline might easily reverse itself. He says that at the time the market crashed a depression could not have been foreseen.

Some other explanations for the crash have been offered, which Galbraith examines. On 20 September a British entrepreneur, Clarence Hatry, was discovered to be a big time fraudster, forging stock certificates and issuing unauthorized stock. This scandal has been seen by some to have hurt confidence in New York and to have sparked off the crash. Another story is that the refusal in early October of the Massachusetts Department of Public Utilities to allow Boston Edison to conduct a stock split , combined with its declaration that the stock was hugely overvalued, caused the panic.

However, according to Galbraith, none of these signals and events satisfactorily explains how the crash began. His view is that it is not important to know how the crash was sparked off, since "… it is in the nature of a speculative boom that almost anything can collapse it."

Despite the market "corrections," in September and October there were still no obvious signs of collapse. Brokers' loans to their customers in September leaped by $670 million, the biggest monthly increase ever. Ivar Kreuger, a reclusive financier who was later discovered to have committed a gigantic fraud, gave an interview to the *Saturday Evening Post* which was generally reassuring. On 15 October Professor Irving Fisher made his famous remark that stocks had reached a "permanently high plateau," adding that, "I expect to see the stockmarket a good deal higher than it is today within a few months."

Nonetheless, a few days later there was another bad break. Doomsayers like the *New York Times* repeated, cautiously, their predictions of a crash. On Monday 21 October the volume of transactions was a little over 6 million, the third largest day in history, says Galbraith. As with prior big days, the ticker fell behind – by noon it was an hour slow and by the end of the day it was off by an hour and 40 minutes. During the boom such lags hadn't mattered much, but now stocks were dropping. The lag made people nervous and encouraged them to sell.

On Thursday 24 October the crash began in earnest. Nearly 13 million stocks changed hands. The markets were in uproar and wild rumors abounded. By midday, a meeting of powerful bankers, including Thomas W. Lamont, senior partner of JP Morgan and Company, and Charles E. Mitchell, the chairman of the National City Bank, decided to pool their resources in an effort to support the market. At 1.30 pm Richard Whitney, then vice-president of the NYSE, appeared on the floor and began to buy stocks on behalf of the pool. The mood changed immediately, and stocks began to go up. By the end of the day there was a net gain of 2 points.

Although people close to Wall Street felt reassured that the bankers had moved in to prevent more stop-loss orders being triggered, across the nation investors were still nervous. All night, brokers' offices stayed open to cope with the mountain of paperwork from the day's business.

For the next two days trading was heavy, but prices were stable. The press reported that the worst was over and applauded the bankers' courageous actions. Everywhere, stuffed shirts made statements of reassurance – the market had settled, the economy was fundamentally sound and so on.

The following Monday, the crisis began again. The market declined further than it had in the whole of the previous week. Late that afternoon the bankers met again. This time there were no promises of support – they had simply discussed how to sell their stockholdings in an orderly manner in order not to increase the panic. Tuesday was even worse; now the investment trusts were hit, many of them were proving unsaleable.

By the end of October, brokers were finding it difficult to borrow money in order to relend for their clients' margins. The New York banks stepped in to help, averting a money panic. On 29 October the NYSE met to discuss closing the exchange; after much discussion they decided to stay open, but to introduce short hours and some special holidays when the market could bear it.

The following day stocks recovered somewhat, recouping most of the previous day's losses. John D. Rockefeller broke several decades of silence to state that, "Believing that the fundamental conditions of the country are sound ... my son and I have for some days been purchasing sound common stocks." This failed to reassure investors.

The investment trusts of the time were heavily leveraged. Now that the stocks they held were dropping in value by 50 percent or more, their value was almost nil or worse. Margin calls were forcing private investors to sell good stocks to keep their holdings of bad ones. Many investment trusts had lent money to brokers to provide margin and had invested in one another – as prices collapsed, the effect on the trusts was magnified, and they exacerbated by buying their own stock in a futile attempt to support the price.

In the first half of November the market continued to slide and it was now generally admitted that things were bad. On Wednesday 13 November, the *New York Times* industrials closed at 224, 50 percent down from 542 on 3 September. President Hoover, elected in 1928, now called meetings on the state of the economy and announced tax cuts. These measures were the most powerful effort yet to reassure the public.

In the spring of 1930 the market recovered, but in June it fell again, continuing downwards through June 1932. In July of that year the New York Times industrials were at 58. The depression had set in.

Galbraith spends the last part of the book examining events in the aftermath of the crash and discussing causes. He argues that the crash itself is easier to explain than the Great Depression that followed it and asserts that the crash did not "cause" the depression. He notes five weaknesses in the economy in 1929:

1. *Unequal distribution of income* – the rich were much richer then than they have been since.
2. *Bad corporate governance* – there was an "exceptional number" of crooks in industry in the 1920s.
3. *A weak banking structure* which allowed a domino effect of failures.
4. *A "dubious" balance of trade position.* During the depression,

Hoover increased import tariffs, making it more difficult for foreign countries to trade their way out of debts already owed to the US.

5. *Bad economic advice.* Galbraith argues that economic policies designed to improve matters only made things worse.

The Great Crash 1929 is an important book for investors. It does not provide easy answers, nor does it overdramatize. It is not racy reading, but does, however, provide a thoughtful and balanced account of what occurred, and reminds us that the world does not come to an end when the stock market goes belly up. For those of us who look to the future, it serves as a useful manual which may help us to survive as investors even in the bleakest times.

HOW TO LIE WITH STATISTICS

by

Darrell Huff

It's all a little like the tale of the roadside merchant who was asked to explain how he could sell rabbit sandwiches so cheap. "Well" he said, "I have to put in some horse meat too. But I mix 'em up fifty-fifty: one horse one rabbit."

(Huff, page 104)

Material quoted within this chapter is extracted from *How to Lie with Statistics* by Darrell Huff, Penguin, London, 1991.

If investors had to pass an exam in statistics before they were allowed to buy stocks, maybe it would put a stop to some of the grosser abuses of this sweet and subtle art. It's an idle thought perhaps, and certainly not in the interests of the institutions, but every new investor does need some sort of inoculation against the many ways in which statistics can be misunderstood or used to deceive. This slim volume provides it.

How to Lie with Statistics was written in 1954 by an American journalist, Darrell Huff, who had a statistical background. Since that time new ways have been found to confuse people with numbers, but the book remains a minor classic, a little gem of skeptical vaccine against the daily torrent of distortions. It is particularly useful when assessing fundamentals, since it is in the worlds of business, politics and the media that statistics are most misused. In his introduction Huff writes:

> "the secret language of statistics ... is employed to sensationalize, inflate, confuse and oversimplify ... without writers who use the words with honesty and understanding and readers who know what they mean, the result can only be semantic nonsense."
>
> *(page 10)*

The book begins with sampling. Samples, you may remember from math classes, are what you have to measure when there are too many of something to count them all. Huff gives the example of a barrel of red and white beans. If you want to discover how many of each type there are, you can find out for certain by counting all the beans. If you had a barrel of millions of beans this would take too long, so you can estimate the proportions of red and white beans by taking a sample from the barrel and counting those – this will give you an approximate answer, but only if the sample you take is representative of the proportions of the two colors in the whole of the barrel (to achieve this you might shake up the barrel to mix the beans before sampling).

Sampling works when the sample is large enough and properly chosen. If one or both of these factors are wrong then the sample will be "biased" and not truly representative of the whole.

Here's one way you might introduce bias accidentally:

- You want to know how many people in the US like answering questionnaires.
- It's too expensive to ask everyone in person, so you decide to send a questionnaire to a number of people which asks "Do you like answering questionnaires?"
- Over the next few weeks some of these people return their questionnaires. To obtain your answer, you decide only to consider these replies.
- Adding them up, you are surprised to find that most of the respondents say that yes, they love answering questionnaires, and so you triumphantly announce that, based on your study, most people in the US enjoy answering questionnaires.

In doing this, says Huff, "you would be following a time-hallowed practice in ignoring [the people who didn't reply] when you announced your findings." In other words, your sample has been biased – people who hate answering questionnaires may have thrown yours away and you have failed to take them into account.

What people say and what they do are not the same thing, which is the trouble with many direct polls. To get at the truth, you have to be sneaky. In the UK, for instance, people who vote for the Conservative Party often lie to pollsters, saying that they vote Labour. This is because, it is said, that Conservatives are afraid of being thought mean, selfish and money-grubbing (which is how their opponents see them). Polls routinely under-estimate the Conservative Party's vote.

People will lie to pollsters about all kinds of things; the book tells of a survey of magazine readership which produced the impossible result that many more people bought and read the middlebrow *Harpers* than the lowbrow *True Story*. It was certain that this was false, since *True Story*'s circulation figures – which were counted, not sampled – were much higher than *Harpers*'. People had lied, perhaps because they were embarrassed to admit what they really liked to read. To get at the truth, the researchers tried another method. They went around houses offering to buy people's old magazines. Even this approach, says Huff, has problems, since it only tells you what people have been "exposed" to, not what they have actually read.

"Oh let us never, never doubt / What nobody is sure about," goes a verse by E.C. Bentley. This is the truth of statistics. You don't know the answer with 100 percent certainty – you are just making estimates and judgements. Sometimes it is possible to test the accuracy by counting the whole "population" (the term for the collection of things you are trying to measure) afterwards, as with the barrel of beans, but often it is not. Much depends on how careful you are in the way you conduct your surveys. In the case of sampling, this means doing your very best to ensure that you ask the right questions (e.g., ones that will reveal the truth) and that you pick a genuinely representative sample.

Here's an example of a famously unsuccessful political poll – believe it or not, the financial markets are sensitive to politics. In 1936 the *Literary Digest* polled 10 million voters who had previously correctly predicted the 1932 Republican victory. In 1936, however, the majority of them said that it would be Landon, not Roosevelt, who would win. How could they be so wrong? It turned out that the sample was biased – those 10 million voters were mainly well-to-do, and thus more likely to vote Republican at any election.

Let's turn to averages, a very loose term. There are three main types of average:

- *the mean*, obtained by dividing the total of the measurements by the number of things measured,
- *the mode*, obtained by seeing which is the most common measurement, and
- *the median*, which is the middle point between the two most extreme measurements.

These numbers are frequently not identical, which gives lots of scope for mistaken and misleading statements. Suppose you are one of the three owner/directors of a business employing 99 people other than the directors, which has had the following result in a salary survey:

per person
employees' wages: $1100
directors' wages: $5500
directors' profits: $7000

The employees aren't going to like this – they're making a miserable $1100 while you're getting a princely $12 500. How are you going to make the figures look better? If you take $15 000 of the $21 000 profit and pay it to the directors as a salary bonus and then include the three directors' salaries when you take a mean average of all wages, you get:

average wage/salary: $1376
average director's profit: $2000

Much better! This is the kind of thing that is the lifeblood of the accounting profession, and, despite all the attempts to regulate and standardize business accounting, the fact is that those who control the management of a business always have scope to adjust their figures to give the best effect. This is why Warren Buffett looks for "honest managers" – he wants to invest in companies where the managers are not perpetually monkeying with the numbers.

If you are interested in finding small capital growth companies, you will inevitably be confronted with the problem of extrapolation. Let's say you are looking at Cyberwidget Inc., which has developed a new high tech product and has only started making sales this year in a test market area of 100 000 people. They've sold 100 units. When the product goes international next year, the market will be, say, of 500 million people, so you might extrapolate and say that next year's sales will be in the same proportion – i.e., 500 000 units. This would be naïve – what about the competition, the increased costs, the regulatory barriers and so on? All these factors, and many more, could combine to make next year's sales considerably less than this extrapolation.

Maybe this is too simple a case to fool anyone, but when it comes to estimating the trend in overall sales in a growing industry, you frequently see this kind of error. Huff describes the market for TV in the early years of the industry – in one five-year period the number of TVs in American homes increased by 10 000 percent. If you extrapolated at the same rate for the next five year period you would get the impossible result that there would be 40 TV sets in every home in America. Speculators in Internet stocks and emerging markets, beware!

Although this book is short, it covers a lot of useful ground – too much to explain it all here. Most usefully of all, the final chapter covers five simple questions to ask yourself when confronted with a statistic:

- *Who says so?* In a Peanuts cartoon Lucy tells Charlie Brown that women scientists have discovered that women are more intelligent than men (one might suspect unconscious bias). A beleaguered industry may produce surveys to "prove" that their products don't kill you, or harm the environment, or whatever, in which case one might suspect conscious bias.

- *How do they know?* Reports of survey results don't always give much detail, but sometimes they will inadvertently reveal that, for instance, the sample taken was extremely small. Try to obtain the real survey results.

- *What's missing?* Look for the type of average used, the standard error, and watch out for changing bases in indices.

- *Did somebody change the subject?* Huff points out that a change in the reported number of cases of something – a disease, say, or crime – is not necessarily the same as a change in the actual number of cases. Maybe the reporting method has changed.

- *Does it make sense?* Extrapolations, as we've seen, are often absurd. Here's another example – "since life expectancy is only 63 years, it is a waste of time to have a social security plan for people over 65, since most people die before that."

In this information age, we investors can't spend our whole time checking the accuracy of other people's surveys – life is just too short. What we can do, though, is familiarize ourselves with statistical method and try to remember that statistical results are only estimates, not definite facts. Try it out – you may be surprised at how many bogus statistical interpretations you find.

THE INTELLIGENT INVESTOR

A BOOK OF PRACTICAL COUNSEL

by

Benjamin Graham

Since our book is not addressed to speculators, it is not meant for those who trade in the market. Most of these people are guided by charts or other largely mechanical means of determining the right moments to buy and sell. The one principle that applies to nearly all these so-called "technical approaches" is that one should buy *because* a stock on the market has gone up and one should sell *because* it has declined. This is the exact opposite of sound business sense everywhere else and it is most unlikely that it can lead to lasting success on Wall Street. In our own stock market experience and observation, extending over 50 years, we have not known a single person who has consistently or lastingly made money by thus "following the market." We do not hesitate to declare that this approach is as fallacious as it is popular.

(Graham, page x)

Material quoted within this chapter is extracted from *The Intelligent Investor: A Book of Practical Counsel* by Benjamin Graham, 4th revised edition, Harper & Row, New York, 1973.

In 1934 a fund manager and part-time academic, Benjamin Graham, produced with his one-time assistant David Dodd, a book called *Security Analysis*. This massive tome has come to be seen as one of the key works that established stock and bond analysis as a professional discipline. It's a dense, difficult book to read but it has remained in print ever since its publication as new generations of Wall Street analysts have drawn on it for an intellectual framework with which to appraise securities.

World War II came and went, and analysts were becoming, if not quite respectable, an established part of Wall Street. Graham decided to write a shorter version of his investment philosophy for the benefit of non-professional investors. This is *The Intelligent Investor*. It, too, is a stodgy volume, wordy and repetitive, but like *Security Analysis* it has enjoyed steady popularity since its publication.

Benjamin Graham is the founder of the approach to the stock-market known as "value investing." At root it is a simple idea. If you buy a company's stock for less than its "true" value – as measured by, say, its per share net asset value – then you have bought a bargain. A $1 book value bought for 40c is still only worth 40c in the market. Graham believed that over time stock price would tend to adjust towards the book value of the company, at which point you could sell at a good profit.

Unlike his famous pupil Warren Buffett, Graham wasn't interested in listed companies as businesses – he didn't concern himself with their products, prospects or plans. After identifying companies with "bargain" prices, his main investment tactic was to ensure that there was a wide margin of safety before he plunged.

In *The Intelligent Investor* Graham points out (it was news at the time) that a way of assessing the margin of safety in a particular stock is to compare its historical rate of return with that of high grade bonds. If good bonds are paying, say, 4 percent a year and the stock's earnings per share are 9 percent of the price paid, the stockholder has a 5 percent margin over the bond rate. If these rates were to stay steady for 10 years, the stockholders' "excess of stock earning power over bond interest may aggregate 50 percent of the price paid." Such a margin, says Graham, is safe and if you were to average your costs by purchasing the stock over several years and diversifying your portfolio, the probability of a good result becomes "very large."

One of the difficulties of reading Graham's books is that they start from first principles: they are nothing if not thorough, but little lip service is paid to other investment views. He is cautious, pedantic and determined to rain on the parade of every first time investor who has ever wanted to make big money fast.

Yet Graham became wealthy through his investments as did many of his students. Says Buffett, "They're all rich now. They haven't invented Federal Express or anything like that. They just set one foot in front of the other. Ben [Graham] put it all down. It's just so simple."

But how can such a miserly approach as value investing be

worthwhile? Such an arm's length, pessimistic view of the world is hardly appealing but perhaps the roots of this safety-first philosophy lie in Graham's formative experiences. He was born in 1894 in London, England to a Polish-Jewish family who took him to New York in the following year. When he was nine his father died, leaving his mother Dora struggling to support her three sons. Dora's business efforts failed and her disastrous attempts to improve her fortunes by trading in odd lots of stock on margin made matters even worse. The young Graham grew up in the knowledge of just how badly investment losses can hurt a family.

Like many other successful investors, Graham started life poor. He was extremely bright and a good student and on graduation was offered teaching posts in no fewer than three departments at Columbia University. He decided to go into Wall Street instead, joining a firm in 1914 and quickly becoming a "statistician," as analysts were then known. By the early 1920s he was a money manager in his own right, acquiring wealth rapidly during the boom. Like almost everyone else he took a bath in the 1929 crash – he'd been cautious, he'd thought, but he'd still been operating the account on a 44 percent margin.

Graham's partnership, now called Graham–Newman, survived the depression by a whisker and began to make money again, but he never forgot the horror of 1929. It is in this context that we must understand *The Intelligent Investor*.

Between 1926 and 1956 Graham–Newman engaged in several types of operation, Graham tells us. They were:

- *"bargain" issues* – the classic value investment approach, of which more below;
- *arbitrages* – Simultaneous buying and selling of related securities during mergers and reorganizations;
- *liquidations* – buying the stock of companies where their assets were to be liquidated and paid out to the stockholders;
- *related hedges* – buying convertibles while selling stock in the same company with the aim of making a profit if the stock's price fell a long way below the price of the convertible;
- *acquisitions* – purchasing a controlling stake in a company.

Of these activities, says Graham, only the hunting for "bargains" is appropriate for non-professional investors. He writes at length about the doubtful accuracy of company accounts where often "fine Italian hands" have been at work, and appears to conclude that in many cases it is simply impossible for an outsider to be sure that the reported figures are accurate. This is the principal reason for the "margin of safety" idea – if you find a company where the stock price is very much lower than its book value, then even vaguely fraudulent or unscrupulous accounting practices should not prevent the investor from making a profit.

Graham offers two basic sets of rules intended for:

- defensive investors
- enterprising investors.

In both cases, Graham advises individuals to hold a proportion of their investment fund in high grade bonds. For defensive investors, he recommends that you either attempt roughly to mimic an index by, say, buying equal numbers of stocks in all 30 constituent members of the Dow Jones Industrial Average, or apply the following rules to stock picking:

1. Choose only companies with more than $100 million in annual sales for an industrial and $50 million for a public utility.
2. Industrials should have their current assets worth at least twice their current liabilities. Long-term debt should not exceed working capital. Utilities' current liabilities should not exceed twice the book value of the company's equity.
3. The company should have some earnings from common stock in each of the last ten years.
4. The company should have a 20-year record (uninterrupted) of dividend payments.
5. The company should have "a minimum increase of at least one-third in per-share earnings in the past ten years using three-year averages at the beginning and end."
6. The present stock price should not be more than 15 times the last three years' average earnings.
7. The stock price should not be more than 1.5 times the last reported book value.

These last two ratios can be varied as long as, when multiplied together, they do not exceed 22.5 – e.g., a company with a price/book value ratio of 2.5 but with a price/earnings ratio of 9 would pass this test.

8. Don't keep fewer than 10 or more than 30 stocks in your portfolio.

For enterprising investors the rules are a little easier:

1. Draw up a list of stocks with low price/earnings ratio – under 9, say.

2. Select companies with current assets at least 1.5 times current liabilities and, for industrials, debt not more than 110 percent of net current assets.

3. Of these, choose the companies that are paying dividends currently.

4. Of these, choose companies with higher earnings last year than they had three years ago.

5. Narrow the list to companies with a stock prices of less than 120 percent of their net tangible assets.

The resulting portfolio is likely to look unappetizing – mainly a bunch of unpopular, unpromising low-cap stocks which look as if they are as cheap as they should be. Graham's point is that, by applying his criteria, you have found bargains; they may be "cigar butts" that someone has thrown away, but you should still get a few good puffs out of them by holding them for a few years.

Value investing is not for everyone, but some people may warm to its frozen-hearted methods – as a value investor you need not read much, like people much or believe much of what you hear. You are not in the business of prediction. You just scour the market for cheapness and hold your bargains until they get up to what you have decided, by mechanical calculation, they are worth. What could be simpler?

JOHN MAYNARD KEYNES

VOLUMES 1 & 2

by

Robert Skidelsky

He was the child of a late-flowering Edwardian Enlightenment which believed – against much evidence, to be sure – that a new age of reason had dawned. The brutality of the closure applied in 1914 helps explain Keynes's reading of the interwar years, and the nature of his mature efforts. This book is about his attempt to restore the expectation of stability and progress in a world cut adrift from its nineteenth-century moorings. He brought in the State to redress the failings of society, not because he loved it, but because he saw it as the last resource. His genius was to have developed an analysis of economic disorder which justified forms of State intervention compatible with traditional liberal values. He was the last of the great English Liberals.

(Skidelsky, page xv)

Material quoted within this chapter is extracted from *John Maynard Keynes, Volume 2, The Economist as Saviour 1920–1937*, by Robert Skidelsky, Macmillan, London, 1992.

As investors, the life and work of J. M. Keynes (pronounced "canes") demands our attention for two very important reasons; firstly, because of his impact as a seminal economist and secondly, because he was a successful speculator himself.

We private investors must of necessity be amateur economists, even if we've had no formal training in "the dismal science." This is not so that we can bore our spouses and friends with endless monologues on the "Big Picture," but simply because a sound understanding of economic forces will serve us well in our pursuit of gains. Economics is the jungle through which we hunt our prey.

Keynes's ideas laid the foundations of Western economic orthodoxy from the late 1940s to the 1970s, although, as with so many other great thinkers, much was subsequently done in his name which he would not have supported. His main practical achievements were to help set up the Bretton Woods system, which helped stabilize currencies after the war, and to provide the intellectual basis for the way in which governments manipulated their own economies during the period that followed.

Keynes's thinking dominated economic policy until the 1970s, when Bretton Woods collapsed, oil prices soared, the system broke down and a new economic orthodoxy emerged – "monetarism." In fact, the "new" orthodoxy of monetarism was in some respects a return to the *"laissez-faire"* ideas of the 19th century, and its own stock has fallen of late with policymakers. What is clear is that, despite the rise and fall of great theories, here is a thinker whose contribution has few equals in the world of economics and finance.

Together, these two volumes make up the latest and best biography of this extraordinary man. Written by Robin Skidelsky, Professor of Political Economics at the University of Warwick, in the UK, they provide a very thorough and thought-provoking examination of Keynes's life and ideas. They are quite brilliantly written and packed full of insights into how the 20th century came to be what it has been. As we move into a new century, and probably a new era, it seems more likely than ever that there will be new revolutions in the global economic system in which we operate. To understand where we are, and what is happening now, we must first understand where we came from and how we got here. Enter the work of Keynes.

Unusually for our select band of "classic" authors, Keynes was born into privilege. Born in 1883, the son of a well-to-do Cambridge academic, he entered several elites early in his life; a brilliant student, he won scholarships to Eton College and to Cambridge and rose high in the British government's Treasury department at a very young age. His investment career began in earnest when, as a fellow of King's College, Cambridge, he made fortunes for both himself and his college through financial speculation during some very tough times.

While a student at Cambridge he joined the Converzazione Society, known as the "Apostles," whose membership included such literary luminaries as Lytton Strachey. The London offshoot of the Apostles became known as the Bloomsbury Group, a loose association of intellectuals, including Virginia Woolf, who rejected their parents' Victorian values, believed in "free love," and had a passion for the literary and visual arts. There is much to dislike about the members of the Bloomsbury Group, but it was important because it brought such giants as Proust, Cézanne, Freud, Dostoevsky, Picasso and Chekhov their deserved recognition in the Anglo-Saxon world. At the same time, Keynes's close friendships with thinkers such as the tortured philosopher Wittgenstein were extremely helpful in the development of his economic theories.

Keynes was the kind of person many people hate. Snobbish, rich, bisexual, privileged, and cunning, he was also, like many very clever people, often rude and generally arrogant. But he was also a radical who was able to change conventions from the inside and succeeded in finding workable solutions to the economic traumas of the Great Depression and the World Wars. To this extent, at least, the world does owe him some thanks.

During World War I Keynes was given his own department in the Treasury and had the ear of the British government at a time when the British Empire was crumbling. Attending the 1919 Versailles Peace Conference, he strongly opposed the swingeing war reparations imposed on Germany by the Allies, but was ignored. Resigning his position in 1920 in order to speak publicly about it, he wrote *The Economic Consequences of the Peace* in which he argued that the reparations were far too high – by a factor of about 10; forcefully attacked the Allied leaders for myopia and correctly predicted that Germany would soon cease its payments and would inevitably want revenge.

Says Skidelsky:

> "everyone agrees that Keynes was 'the most intuitive of men,' using 'intuitive' as people talk, or used to talk, of 'feminine' intuition – as something apart from rationality ... More interesting is the privileged epistemic status Keynes claimed for intuition in general, and his intuitions in particular ... He regarded an economic argument ... as, in the first instance, a way of exposing the 'intuitions' of those taking part ... As with all original minds, Keynes's intuitions were never fully captured by his analytical system. His books are full of historical generalizations which are not 'modeled' at all. And his theory of liquidity hardly captures the richness and passion of his informal speculations concerning the psychology of hoarding or his view that 'love of money' was the cancer of economies."

(page xix)

It is this intuitive side of Keynes that makes him so different from many of today's spouters of economic theory. He certainly did not believe that you could nail the complexities of economic life down into a neat theoretical system.

Deep down, Keynes wanted states to intervene in economic affairs because he saw the horrific effects of mass unemployment during the interwar period. He may have been a liberal, but he also believed in capitalism as the best system – unlike some of his followers! During times of great unemployment he thought that it was wrong for the rich to hang on to their wealth at all costs; if they spent money it would stimulate business and people would be able to get jobs. During his lifetime, this seems to me to have been a radical and inspired solution; today, when the West is no longer full of war-widows, traumatized soldiers and the miserably poor, he perhaps would have adapted his views. Possibly his greatest contribution was to show (like Marx) that modern capitalist economies are basically unstable – to keep them on track, they have to be controlled to some extent.

The book is not merely a discussion of his theories. It also tells the story of his life, and there are many charming episodes. Having been an active homosexual during his early life, he suddenly fell in love with one of Diaghilev's ballet dancers, Lydia Lopokova, marrying her in 1925. Some of his friends disapproved strongly – Virginia Woolf hated the idea that he was married to a "parrokeet," while Clive Bell "used to say that her spiritual home was Woolworths." The half-mad Wittgenstein made her cry when she said, "What a beautiful tree!" by responding fiercely, "What exactly do you mean?" In short, this lively, free-spirited Russian was treated unkindly by his friends because she was not as clever as they were. But Lydia won; Keynes's marriage to her was extremely successful, productive and loving, perhaps because he needed someone completely different from himself.

In the course of a long life, Keynes had many ups and downs as an investor, too numerous to detail here. What is interesting about him is that he made money in the markets and did other more important things, unlike some of the other investors we look at in this book. He was, you might say, more of a Soros than a Buffett, using his knowledge of the world to make profits rather than concentrating on the qualities of individual businesses alone. In 1929 he was almost wiped out and two years later unsuccessfully tried to sell two of his best paintings, a Matisse and a Seurat, but by 1936 he had made the equivalent of $21 million in today's money, speculating on Wall Street.

In the 1920s he played with currencies and commodities, trying to beat the market short term. As he matured, he decided that credit cycle investment was a loser's game and concentrated on a few favorite stocks, buying more when the market fell. Of investment, Keynes said, "It is the one sphere of life and activity where victory, security and success is always to the minority and never to the majority. When you find anyone agreeing with you, change your mind. When I can persuade the Board of my Insurance Company [where he was a director] to buy a share, that, I am learning from experience, is the right moment for selling it."

There are no quick lessons to be learned from these two volumes, no little ruses to improve your investment performance; they are books to study over a period, to read slowly, to borrow from the library several times over. If you can get to grips with them, you'll have a profound insight into the world that only a minority have acquired – and, as Keynes said, to win at investment you have to be in the minority!

LIAR'S POKER
TWO CITIES, TRUE GREED

by

Michael Lewis

My client loved risk. Risk, I had learned, was a commodity in itself. Risk could be canned and sold like tomatoes. Different investors place different prices on risk. If you are able, as it were, to buy risk from one investor cheaply, and sell it to another investor dearly, you can make money without taking any risk yourself. And this is what we did.

(Lewis, page 220)

Material quoted within this chapter is extracted from *Liar's Poker: Two Cities, True Greed* by Michael Lewis, Hodder & Stoughton, 1989.

Liar's Poker is the story of Michael Lewis's experience as a bond trader for Salomon Brothers between 1985 and 1988. The title comes from a game the traders used to play, bidding on the serial numbers of dollar bills. John Gutfreund, Salomon's CEO, once challenged John Meriwether, a star bond trader, to one hand of "liar's poker" for one million dollars. Even by Salomon's standards this was excessive. Meriwether was in a quandary. If he won, his boss would be upset. If he lost – well, who wants to lose a million dollars on one lousy bet? But he couldn't back down – that wasn't an option in Salomon's gung-ho corporate culture. Instead, Meriwether upped the ante to 10 million dollars. Gutfreund politely declined.

Maybe this kind of thing is common enough in Las Vegas, but Wall Street professionals, and the staff at Salomon Brothers in particular, were not gamblers – they were out to make money. Prior to the 1980s, few people knew much about Salomon's business, which was bond trading. This was, says Lewis, partly because educated people did not become bond traders – they preferred to become low-paid investment bank analysts because, says Lewis, they wanted to be thought succesful by people like themselves. In 1968 13 of Salomon's 28 partners didn't have a college degree and one had not completed the eighth grade. But in the 1980s all this began to change, following the Federal Reserve's decision in late 1979 to fix the money supply and allow interest rates to fluctuate. This decision had the effect of greatly increasing the volatility of bond prices, enabling Salomon Brothers, with its specialized expertise, to make a killing.

The basic business was straightforward. A large company would borrow money by issuing its own paper – corporate bonds – and Salomon would sell these to the lenders, their customers (principally financial institutions), and take a small cut on each deal. If the institution wished to sell its bonds, Salomon would find another buyer, effectively making a market in the securities. Lewis writes:

> "For most of its life Salomon had been a scrappy bond-trading house distinguished mainly by its ability to and willingness to take big risks. Salomon had to accept risk to make money because it had no list of fee-paying corporate clients, unlike, say, the genteel Gentiles of Morgan Stanley. The image Salomon had projected to the public was of a firm of clannish Jews, social nonentities, shrewd but honest, sinking its nose more deeply into the bond markets than any other firm cared to. This was a caricature, of course, but it roughly captured the flavor of the place as it once was."

Making vast profits in the early 1980s, Salomon greatly expanded its staff. When he graduated from the London School of Economics in 1984, Lewis was just one of thousands of well-educated people who wanted to get their hands dirty in finance, but he was getting rejected by every firm he applied to. By chance he was invited to a corporate dinner in St James's Palace, London, for insurance salesmen, presided over by the Queen

Mother, and spent the evening being quizzed by the wife of one of Salomon's managing directors. She liked him and promised to get him a job. As the Queen Mother proceeded past them on her way out, the woman yelled, "Hey, Queen, nice dogs you have there!" This was Lewis's introduction to Salomon's crude, rambunctious ways.

Lewis is at his best when describing the characters and shenanigans of the trading floor. Take, for instance, the "Human Piranha," inventor of Salomon's finest accolade, the "Big Swinging Dick." To get to be a "Big Swinging Dick" you had to make big sales on behalf of the firm – it didn't matter if you were male or female – and the award was announced over loudspeakers in the trading room. The Human Piranha, a Harvard graduate, talked in "Fuckspeak" – "If you don't pay fuckin' attention to the fuckin' two year [bonds], you get your fuckin' face ripped off," he'd snarl at an awed room of trainees. The majority of trainees did not survive the course – which was intentional – either being booted out or ending up in peripheral jobs. For the trainees, the worst job you could get was selling equities in Dallas.

Lewis managed to stay the distance and get onto the trading floor as a "geek," ... "a disgusting larval stage between trainee and man." Geeks were much abused; one kid, named Matty, was forced to spend most of his days carrying huge quantities of food from the canteen to the trading floor where it was devoured by obese and gluttonous traders. One trader would eat 20 dollars' worth of candy every afternoon, in addi-

tion to the mountains of burgers, fries, colas, cookies and piz-
zas that would appear in a near-continuous stream all day,
starting at 8 am.

One day Matty didn't pay for the food, and boasted about it to
one of the traders. That afternoon he received a call from someone who said they worked for a special projects division of the
SEC. He was investigating the report of a theft from Salomon's
canteen. Matty laughed it off and put the phone down. The next
day his boss called him into his office, where he was forced to
admit the theft and left to sweat until the following morning,
when he was summoned before the CEO, John Gutfreund, an
unheard-of event.

Gutfreund gave him a long, scary lecture and told him he
could stay on, for now. Matty returned, ashen-faced, to his desk,
convinced that the incident would dog him for the rest of his
career. The traders started laughing. It had all been a practical
joke. Matty burst into tears and ran out of the building. Later he
was persuaded to come back; he'd passed the initiation test.

Salomon's practical jokes did not end with the geeks – they
would play them on other Wall Street firms too. As it became
more and more clear to the rest of the world that they were
making a fortune, other firms began to poach their traders
for enormous salary increases. Merrill Lynch offered Ron
Dipasquale, an inexperienced trader, a million dollars a year,
guaranteed for two years. He signed, and within a week Merrill
Lynch had discovered its mistake. Normally Salomon would

never take a defector back, but after twiddling his thumbs for two years at Merrill Lynch, Dipasquale returned to a standing ovation at Salomon and subsequently distinguished himself as a trader.

Lewis himself suffered as a geek. Based in London, his job was to sell US bonds to European speculators. "There was good reason for their eagerness," he writes. "The American bond market was going through the roof. Imagine how crowds would overwhelm a casino in which everyone who plays wins big and you'll have some idea what our unit was like in those days." Lewis didn't know what he was doing at first, and more experienced traders would offload overpriced bonds on him, to sell to naïve customers like Helmut, the employee of an Austrian bank, for whom Lewis rapidly lost $150 000.

Gradually he began to wise up. "Customers have very short memories," intoned one of his bosses, supporting the ethos of screwing customers when necessary. Lewis discovered a Frenchman who was willing to buy the bonds of Olympia & York, a property company owned by the reclusive Reichmann brothers which later got into trouble. Lewis was unsure whether to sell him the bonds – to make his customer a profit, Lewis would have to buy them back and "stick someone else's customer with them." Eventually he made the sale, worth $86 million, and sat back, feeling guilty. The phone rang. It was the Human Piranha, yelling, "That is fuckin' awesome. I mean fuckin' awesome. I fuckin' mean fuckin' awesome. You are one

Big Swinging Dick and don't let anybody tell you different."
Michael Lewis had finally arrived.

The writing was on the wall, however. Competition from
other firms became more intense, and after the 1987 crash and
the Boesky and Milken scandals, Salomon's glory days were
over. Lewis left the firm at the beginning of 1988 having, he says,
"lost my need to stay." Having left the great game he published
the book in 1989.

Liar's Poker has subsequently been attacked in many quarters
but the fact remains that back in those heady days trading was
the way he describes. Its hilarious and unnerving insights into
the lives of some of finance's most highly paid players should
not be lost on any investor, and for my money, this has to be the
best book to come out of the financial world of the late 1980s. It
captures the "greed is good" spirit of the times in Wall Street and
the City and serves as an object lesson to all those who believe
that *all* financial professionals *always* look after their customers.
Sit tight and enjoy the ride!

16

MARKET WIZARDS
INTERVIEWS WITH TOP TRADERS

by

Jack D. Schwager

Trading provides one of the last great frontiers of opportunity in our economy. It is one of the very few ways in which an individual (such as those interviewed here) succeed in turning this feat, but at least the opportunity exists.

(Schwager, page x)

Material quoted within this chapter is extracted from *Market Wizards: Interviews with Top Traders* by Jack D. Schwager, HarperCollins, New York, 1993.

Futures trading is a "zero-sum game," says one of the interviewees in this rollicking collection of question and answer sessions with the desperados of the financial world, derivatives traders.

You have to respect them. In a game where only a small fraction manage to avoid total loss (estimates in the book vary from 2 percent to 1 percent), these men – sadly, they *are* all men in the book – must be doing something right. Efficient marketeers, naturally, would seek to explain trading success by chance, but not one of the people interviewed regards the market as efficient.

This is about the only point that they agree on. Their methods, backgrounds and investment views are extraordinarily diverse. "Technical analysis, I think, has a great deal that is right and a great deal that is mumbo-jumbo," opines Bruce Korner, a trader in the currency markets who handles hundreds of millions of dollars, while other interviewees, equally successful, read charts obsessively.

Michael Marcus, who principally trades commodities, appears to have only just discovered the use of ratio analysis for stock assessment:

"I like to use something I found in the *Investor's Daily*, the earnings per share (EPS) ... I also like to look at the price/earnings (P/E) ratio in conjunction with the EPS .... In other words, while I like to see a company with a strong earnings growth pattern, I also want to know how much the market is paying for that earnings growth pattern."

(*page 47*)

Who doesn't?

Not William O'Neil, the founder of the *Investor's Daily* (where Marcus found EPS), and a successful stock investor. He thinks that "there is a very low correlation between the P/E ratios and the best performing stocks ... A common mistake ... is to buy a stock because the P/E ratio looks cheap."

Not so, thinks "treasure hunter" David Ryan: "O'Neil says the P/E ratio is not important. I think it is, in that your success ratio is a lot higher on lower P/E ratio stocks."

Traders do not have the highest of reputations. As the gunslingers of the financial world, they are often seen as hot-shots, battling daily against insurmountable odds. The interviewees in this book come over as quite sane, however. There are several ex-scholars amongst them and they all have extremely complex and individual ways of trying to make sense of the markets. This should not be a surprise; surviving in this riskiest of all businesses, and it is a business at the level these traders play it, requires self-reliance. This is no game for dumb, timid people, dumb, brave people or smart, timid people – you have to be brave and smart.

The traders interviewed operate in many markets, including commodities, currencies, stocks, bonds and futures. The futures markets have grown enormously during the last few decades – the author estimates that in 1988, futures contracts traded in the US alone were worth more than $10 trillion.

What's a future? Essentially it is a contract to buy or sell, at an agreed price on a future date, anything from pork bellies to the interest rates on bonds. The simple gamble is that on that future date the difference between the price you paid and the current market price ("spot" price) will be in your favor. If you are a producer of the item concerned, a futures contract can help you to hedge against price fluctuations and keep your business stable. If you're a speculator, and these traders are, then you will almost never take delivery of the goods – you are speculating on the prices alone.

In this abstract world, there are a number of factors which encourage speculation. The author enumerates these as:

- *Standardized contracts.* This makes trading easy.
- *High liquidity.* Except in certain circumstances (see below) you can deal at any time during market hours.
- *Short selling is easy.* It's easier than in the stockmarket, where you must borrow stock to go short (*see* page 13).
- *High leverage.* This, Schwager points out, is what gives the futures markets their reputation for high risk. A trader has, initially, only to supply 5 percent to 10 percent of the contract value in order to trade.
- *Low dealing costs.* Schwager says that because costs are so low it is cheaper to offset a risk on stockholdings by taking a counter position in the futures markets than it is to sell the stocks. This is one of George Soros's favorite moves (*see* pages 193–201).
- *Guaranteed transactions.* All deals are guaranteed by the clear-

ing house, so traders need not worry about the financial soundness of their colleagues, which may vary minute by minute throughout the day.

Some futures markets have a limit on daily price changes. If the price moves to the upper limit, the market locks "limit up" and if the price goes to the lower limit it locks "limit down." This rule has the effect that trading almost ceases when the market is locked, and this situation can continue for several days or more, leaving losers trapped in their positions.

Some traders have seats on exchanges – purchased at a high price – which, amongst other advantages, gives them the right to trade *mano a mano* in the pit. Floor trading gives you an immediate, physical sense of the fluctuating mood of the market. Most floor traders live by "scalping," which means taking very small profits on transactions, often buying and selling instantaneously. Others prefer to trade from their desks, watching computer screens and operating in several markets at once.

Not all of the individuals interviewed admit to being traders at all. Jim Rogers, for instance, one-time partner of George Soros, says, "I often hold positions for years. Furthermore, I'm probably one of the world's worst traders. I never get in at the right time."

He gives the example of selling gold short during a massive advance in 1979–80. He sold short at $675 and watched the price go up by nearly $200. Rogers held on, sure that the price rise was "something that couldn't last. It was the gold market's dying gasp." Four days later he was proved correct. Four days! For most of us this is a short time, but to a trader it is an eternity.

Rogers is a fundamentalist and a student of political economy. He tries to think about what will happen in six months' to two years' time. In this respect he is unlike the other traders in the book – he is very internationally-minded and is forever on the lookout for anomalous situations across a very wide range of markets. In 1982 he decided that the German stock market was ready for a boom (there hadn't been one since 1961) following the elections which, he believed, would be won by a party that favored investment.

Having come to that conclusion, Rogers did not take a great deal of trouble in selecting stocks – he simply bought a number of them (presumably large companies) and held them for three years as the German market shot up.

At about the same time, Rogers was watching the Kuwaiti stock market, which was enjoying a wild bull run fueled by easy credit – you could buy any amount of stock with post-dated checks. On the face of it this was a perfect opportunity to go short but Rogers chose not to do so, certain that when the market did collapse the rules would be changed so that he could not get his money out. "One of the best rules anyone can learn about investing is to do nothing, absolutely nothing, unless there is something to do," says Rogers.

Contrast this approach with that of Michael Marcus, who has operated as both a floor trader and a desk trader. He gave up floor trading but says you can earn a lot from it. "You develop an almost subconscious sense of the market on the floor. You learn to gauge price movements by the intensity of the voices in the ring."

For Marcus, the study of intraday chart prices is important. At one time, he says, he was able to predict short-term movements from these charts, but now the markets have changed. Based in California, he says that the markets are ever-evolving but that it is possible to adapt your strategy successfully to new conditions. He is willing to act on slim hints. When he saw on TV that Afghanistan had been invaded by the Russians, he called Hong Kong and discovered that no-one there seemed to have heard the news, so he bought 200 000 ounces of gold. "Then, when the news broke about five to ten minutes later, everybody started scrambling. I had an immediate $10 per ounce profit on 200 000 ounces." $2 million in a few minutes from watching TV! Marcus has subsequently been advised not to visit the gold floor in Hong Kong, where he is not remembered with affection.

This is a fascinating book about a heady world. Although many of the interviewees appear to use techniques which they keep secret, presumably so as not to alert their rivals, they do their best to describe this high-risk, high-pressure life.

A die-hard trader is perhaps not very capable at longer-term investing. The action, the speed at which an endless succession of deals flows through their hands, seems to be what makes them tick. "Money," they seem to say, "is not our primary motivation." I conclude the following:

- If you are a born trader, you'll know it. Maybe you should get a job on an exchange.
- If you are not an experienced investor, stay away from this crazy game.
- If you are an experienced investor, there is some scope for increasing your profits by the judicious use of futures, in the mode of a longer-term thinker like Jim Rogers. Biding your time and picking your opportunities carefully is vital.

All investors have a love affair with risk – as this book shows, in some cases it becomes a veritable orgy of promiscuity!

THE MONEY GAME

by

Adam Smith

... I called up my favorite roomful of gunslingers, who were busy trading stocks to each other. I told them we better be wary of the market, there is a cloud up there no bigger than a man's hand, the transistor radios stolen from the GIs are turning into gold in London, and those Pakistan Airlines planes are carrying it right to Peking. My friend Charley said I was crazy.

"Come on down," he said. "We bought a stock yesterday that's up twenty-five percent today. Listen to the tape. Enjoy, enjoy."

"I have just told you we were heading for a gold crisis," I said. "I have it from a card-carrying member of *Geldarbeitgeschrei* Number Eleven, William McChesney Martin's ball boy."

"Forget it," Charley said. "The gold bugs have been around forever. The market still has gas. Who understands gold anyway? And how can you worry about something you can't understand?"

(Smith, page 235)

Material quoted within this chapter is extracted from *The Money Game* by Adam Smith, Random House, Inc., New York, 1976.

"Adam Smith" is a pseudonym, they say, for a fund manager and journalist named George J.W. Goodman. *The Money Game*, first published in 1967, is a delightfully written exploration of the nature of investment, its quandaries and controversies, and, most of all, its connection with human psychology. Much of the book consists of anecdotes about the markets because, says the author, stories "always teach more than rules."

The Money Game hasn't really dated. Some of the preoccupations may seem a little 1960s now – the easy references to Jung, Freud, Zen and Alan Watts (a writer on Oriental philosophy who was much in vogue during the flower power era) reflect a softer, more eclectic mood than we allow ourselves today. The meat of the book and the serious points that it makes, however, are perennial.

What is the aim of the book? Says Adam Smith, it is "not a how-to-do-it book. Any book that is merely about some technique for manipulating securities can be expected to fade once the technique is popular. We have had books that say, buy assets. That worked for a time. Books that say, convertible bonds. Fine until collapse. Books that say (even as this one does), find rapidly growing companies ..."

Smith's goal here is to give the private investor a revealing insight into, and genuine sense of, the complexity of the markets, and the kinds of rewards you can realistically expect. At the heart of this classic is Smith's observation that if you don't know about yourself, then "the market is an expensive place to find out."

Adam Smith is interested in the human personality. He says that whether you are a private investor or a successful fund manager, your portfolio will tend to reflect your own emotions and prejudices. You may have a tendency to hold on for too long to certain types of growth stock, say, or to avoid the high flyers of the day. Indeed, some institutions will switch their managers periodically from one fund to another for this very reason.

Private individuals, with no clients to answer to, can develop all manner of quirks and odd individual preferences that manifest in their investment choices. To illustrate this, he recounts a series of lunches he had with patients of a psychiatrist friend who were also investors. There is a woman who will only hold one stock and loves it like a child, knowing nothing of its fundamentals. Then there's the man who inherited $2 million worth of stock and feels guilty about it – he enjoys making profits in his own business, but stock investing just seems too easy.

Another man talks like a loser but is actually highly successful. He berates himself for selling too soon and calls himself stupid for not having bought more when one of his stocks goes up. Smith thinks he's made about 500 percent on his stake and says of him that "I suppose some people are only really happy with motherly sympathy, and sometimes it gets hard to find a reason for Mother to be sympathetic."

The best story is of a stockbroker's Grandma, a wealthy little old lady, who persuades him to open a speculative account for her, kept secret from the rest of the family. She's successful, and starts to pass on his tips to her elderly girlfriends. The grandson discovers a small company with great potential but not much stock in issue. He puts his Grandma into it and says she can tell one or two of her friends about it. All of a sudden the stock starts getting hard to buy. He inquires discreetly around Wall Street, but the professionals don't know about it. Some tycoon must be accumulating the stock. Then he has a brainstorm and calls Grandma, who admits that she's told quite a few of her friends about the company – a gang of little old ladies are ramping the stock up in a big way.

The broker is exasperated; she shouldn't be in speculative stocks anyway. Grandma, who is 80, says she has to own growth companies so she can build up a stake for her old age. He threatens to stop giving her tips.

> "When you're 80," Grandma said quietly, "it gets lonely. I bore you all, I know that. And I want my friends to call me. This is the most fun I've had in years. Don't take my stocks away."
>
> "What could I say?"
>
> *(page 65)*

What Smith does say in *The Money Game* is that you can't make big money in the markets as an outsider. Sure, you can make a lousy million dollars, or multiply your money 10 or 20 times, but the really big payoffs go to people who build up a business and then float it on the market. His friend Max, son of immigrants, has done just this: so Adam Smith asks him how his new wealth has changed his life. Max replies that it hasn't made much difference, except that it has made his father happy. His father now knows that he was right when, long ago in another country, he thought that America's streets were paved with gold.

Adam Smith has a big heart and a nice sense of humor. His view of the market is essentially fundamentalist; he likes growth stocks and recommends Philip Fisher (*see* pages 71–81). Interestingly, he says that Fisher's famous "scuttlebutt" method (*see* page 73) only produced one-sixth of his successful stock picks. The rest came from a few really smart and well-informed specialists. This, I submit, is not surprising since in many businesses you start by networking and end up by concentrating on a few key relationships with high-performing allies.

The author regards chartism as flawed but points out that it cannot cop out the way fundamental analysts often do when a recommendation is falling flat, by saying that it will make a good long-term investment. He gives credence to the random walkers (*see* pages 175–183) and supports this with Keynes's statement that the market is a little like a game of musical chairs, where every player knows that at some point the music will stop and someone will have nowhere to sit.

"I think the market is both a game and a Game, i.e., both sport, frolic, fun and play, and a subject for continuously measurable options. If it is a game, then we can relieve ourselves of some of the heavy and possibly crippling emotions that individuals carry into investing, because in a game where the winning of the stake is so clearly defined, Anything else becomes irrelevant."

This is essentially his position; enjoy the game, or don't play it. Perhaps one day, he speculates, the world will be a better place and money seeking will no longer be important. In the mean time, play the game if you want to, or spend your time on other, equally rewarding things. It's your choice.

THE MONEY MASTERS/
THE NEW MONEY
MASTERS

by

John Train

I might say that there's no luck to professional portfolio investing. It is a craft, involving thousands of decisions a year. You can no more pile up a superlative record by luck or accident than you can win a chess tournament by luck or accident. A single individual may well have a lucky strike, but to the year-in, year-out manager of a diversified portfolio, no one event is likely to make an overwhelming difference.

(Train, page xx)

Material quoted within this chapter is extracted from *The New Money Masters* by John Train, HarperCollins, New York, 1990.

About 20 years ago I read John Train's *Preserving Capital and Making It Grow* (originally published as *The Dance of the Money Bees*), and it changed my life. For the first time I encountered a rational, sophisticated view of money – not just how to make it, but how to use it as well and, most importantly of all, how to keep it. His was an authentic voice; you could tell, even if you were as ignorant as I was then, that the author was no snake oil salesman, nor was he some deluded get-rich-quick obsessive who thought that making money in the markets was a cinch.

What's more, he was funny. He told good stories and he told them well. He made you feel that you too could penetrate the mysteries of finance if you tried hard enough.

The Money Masters and its sequel, *The New Money Masters*, are collections of short essays on a gallery of individuals who have made great fortunes in the markets. Bestsellers both, the books are in some ways the victims of their own success. First, by popularizing successful investment methods, such as "value investing," they have helped to dilute the effectiveness of the very techniques they seek to reveal. Second, by awakening a huge interest in such investment icons as Benjamin Graham and Warren Buffett they have spawned a plethora of other books about these personalities which explain their lives and operations in much more detail. A number of the investors featured have written their own books, before or subsequently, such as Philip Fisher (*see* pages 71–81) Peter Lynch (*see* pages 41–47) and Jim Rogers.

Occasionally the books' topicality becomes redundant. The essays are based on interviews and reading about what was on someone's mind regarding, say, oil prices 15 years ago is not particularly fascinating. Nevertheless these two volumes provide an excellent introduction to the methods of some of America's finest, most enduring, investors.

Reassuringly, John Train is himself a money manager. He founded Train, Smith Investment Counsel in New York, specializing in handling the assets of high net worth families. By all accounts he is, like the men about whom he writes, a successful investor but we hear little of this in his books. What he does tell us about himself is generally self-deprecating, such as his confession that, decades ago, he missed a trick by refusing to invest with the young Warren Buffett because he didn't like Buffett's secretive terms (*see* page 56).

It is because of his experience as an investment counsellor that Train is able to act so effectively as a guide and interpreter for the reader. What works well for a professional managing a fund with hundreds of millions of dollars is not necessarily going to work for you and me, private investors with less money, time and resources available to us. But however limited our own resources may be at the moment, it is still important to be aware of techniques that we will probably never use, such as George Soros's bizarre multimarket speculations, Stanley Kroll's commodity trading or Peter Lynch's omnivorous appetite for data. Train explains what techniques private investors can actually apply for themselves.

In *The New Money Masters* there is a chapter of particular value because it examines a topic that is rarely discussed – what to do with your millions once you have made them, and how to pass them on to future generations. It's called "Old Money."

Train contends that vast fortunes cannot be preserved indefinitely – that is, for centuries. Eventually a rich family will lose its wealth and merge back into the mass of humanity. To grasp this, think of the Imperial and senatorial families of ancient Rome – how many of their descendants have managed to retain their wealth for two millennia?

Well, there are a few rich Italians today who claim descent from Roman senators, but broadly the answer is "none." Train describes the process thus:

> "The rest of society yearns to erase the claim on it represented by your capital, and pursues that objective unremittingly, through tax, inflation, regulation, labor demands and other weapons. In this unending duel between the saver and society, society almost always wins in time. Most family fortunes are eventually undermined, given enough time."
>
> *(page 97)*

I would put it more strongly – **all** family fortunes are eventually undermined, period.

Train tells the story of the Rockefeller family, whose 80 members have their affairs managed by a staff of 200 in an office suite in Rockefeller Center known as "Room 5600." John D. Rockefeller Jr, the son of the dynasty's founder, set up five trusts for his children in 1934 which control most of Rockefeller Group Inc. Train's book was first published in 1989, at which time Rockefeller Group had four principal subsidiaries which controlled the Rockefeller Center real estate, worth $1.6 billion, other real estate worth around $1 billion, Venrock Associates, a venture capital operation and various other operations.

Later generations of rich families are usually unlike their forefathers; they are often unworldly (a trait which the family trust office unwittingly tends to encourage) and frequently have very different values – what Train calls "the Patty Hearst syndrome." This explains the main purpose of trusts – to prevent later generations from squandering their money too rapidly. The trouble is that trust managers tend not to be great investors (they're better at law and accounting) and they are extremely expensive to feed. In 1983 it was discovered that the income on the total assets of Rockefeller Group was only 1 percent annually; the situation was eventually corrected, but it serves as a reminder that even the very, very rich can start losing money if they take their eyes off the ball.

"Revocable" trusts, which allow the beneficiaries to call the shots, are often preferred by the wealthy – although you can undo them if you wish, Train says that people rarely do so:

> "… it interposes a level of control, a brake, between the individual and the fortune. 'HAVE FOUND ENCHANTING VILLA IN BARILOCHE,' cables the excited beneficiary, 'ONLY $200,000,

REDUCED FROM $400,000.' 'UNWISE,' cables back the trustee gloomily. The grantor could just dissolve the trust and buy the chalet, but somehow rarely does. An even better example is the imprudent girl beneficiary who becomes enamored of a Greek playboy on the Riviera. He wants her to put $800,000 into a marina on Corfu or a game lodge in Kenya. 'I'd love to, Iannis,' breathes the infatuated damsel, 'but I've got to ask the Office.' 'Why?' demands her admirer, 'Can't you just do what you want? It's your money, isn't it?' 'Oh, but I have to,' she replies. 'We always ask the Office.' Rightly! By the time the trustees' squad of glassy-eyed deal-killers have brought realism to the cash-flow projections and redone the legal arrangements, our young lady should discover whether Iannis is really interested in her or just her bank account."

(pages 106–107)

The point about money is that you have to really, really want to make it grow, and be prepared to dedicate your life to doing so, in order to achieve your aims. If you're born rich, you may quite sensibly have better things to do – which is perhaps why most great investors start poor.

These are books that every new investor should read. Study them yourself, and give them to your kids when they're 18; they give an very accurate picture of just what it takes to get rich as an investor.

A RANDOM WALK DOWN WALL STREET

by

Burton G. Malkiel

Investing requires a lot of work, make no mistake about it. Romantic novels are replete with tales of great family fortunes lost through neglect or lack of knowledge on how to care for money. Who can forget the sounds of the cherry orchard being cut down in Chekhov's great play? Free enterprise, not the Marxist system, caused the downfall of Chekhov's family. They had not worked to keep their money ...

... Most important of all, however, is the fact that investing is *fun*. It's fun to pit your intellect against that of the vast investment community and to find yourself rewarded with an increase in assets. It's exciting to review your investment returns and to see how they are accumulating at a faster rate than your salary. And it's also stimulating to learn about new ideas for products and services, and innovations in the form of financial investments. A successful investor is generally a well-rounded individual who puts a natural curiosity and an intellectual interest to work to earn more money.

(Malkiel, pages 26 and 27)

Material quoted within this chapter is extracted from *A Random Walk Down Wall Street* by Burton G. Malkiel, W. W. Norton, New York, 1991.

Most investment books are about how to make money. This one is principally about the nature of the market itself. It's written by an academic, Burton G. Malkiel, who is Chemical Bank Chairman's Professor of Economics at Princeton University. Don't be put off, though – the book is clearly written and easy to read.

Malkiel discusses the theoretical bases for the major approaches to investment and explores their strengths and flaws. This is a boon to investors; most people get into the market in a haphazard way and pick up bits of knowledge as they go along. In general, if you are a private investor you'll adopt a strategy that appeals to you and feels right – this is sensible, but if that is all you do, you'll never get to the heart of the big question, which is "How do the stock markets really work?"

Most people want easy answers or, at the very least, definite ones. The stockmarket will not yield to this demand – it is a vastly complex phenomenon with a mystifying ability to change the way it behaves over time. A rule that worked well for, say, 30 years may suddenly become useless. A strategy which appears to make perfect sense may lose you money. You aren't going to get any easy explanations of why this is so, but if you are prepared to live with the many paradoxes that seem innate in the workings of the market then you should read this book.

Malkiel contrasts two main philosophical approaches to stocks: the "castles in the air" view and the "firm foundation" view. "Castles in the air" refers to the insight that when a stock becomes popular its price goes up – thus, an investors might try to seek out those stocks that appeared to be becoming increasingly popular in the hope that others would follow later, driving up the price. Technical analysis, or "chartism," offers various systems which attempt to exploit this phenomenon. The problem is that investors' appetites for a given stock are not infinite. Eventually the prices will simply seem too high, short-term stockholders will take their profits and the price will drop.

The "firm foundation" philosophy sees stock prices as being related to the "fundamental" value of the companies that they represent. Thus, if a business increases its profits and the value of its assets, it becomes worth more to its stockholders and eventually the stock price will adjust upwards to reflect this. Firm foundation's practical strategy is "fundamental analysis," the art of scrutinizing businesses and attempting to estimate their present and future worth.

While both these views may be based on genuine insights into market behavior, neither are completely satisfactory. They do not fully explain how stock prices move, nor do they allow investors to apply methods that will work consistently.

Technical analysis is easy to demolish. Its premise that there are repeating patterns in the movements of stock prices which can be recognized and used to make profits consistently can be shown to be generally false. In its most extreme form chartism is an occult art. In fact, W.D. Gann (see pages 99–104), one of the great chartists, was something of an astrologer and magician.

Malkiel tells us that the idea that there is momentum in stock price movement is false. He says that exhaustive studies of price data on both of the major exchanges (NYSE and NASDAQ) going back to the turn of the century "reveal conclusively that past movements of stock prices cannot be used to foretell future movements. The central proposition of charting, therefore, is absolutely false and investors who follow its precepts will accomplish nothing but increasing substantially the brokerage charges they pay." These statistical studies are cited in the book's excellent bibliography if you wish to go into the numbers in detail.

Malkiel points out that random number sequences, such as those that you get by flipping a coin many times, produce what are apparently meaningful patterns but are actually the results of pure chance. A long run of "heads" or "tails" has no effect on the result of the next flip – one flip of a coin is not related to the result of any other flip, so any apparent trend is an illusion.

A way to measure the success of technical analysis is simply to compare it with a "buy and hold" strategy for the same stocks. Studies show that a randomly selected portfolio of stock bought and held for 60 years has produced an annual return of roughly 1 percent. Technical analysis ought to beat this rate over the same period to be worthwhile – but, says Malkiel, it doesn't.

Some popular investment methods don't appear to be "technical" at first glance. For example, "relative strength" systems, such as the one proposed by Michael O'Higgins (*see* pages 29–40) require the investor to buy and hold stocks which have been outperforming general market indices in the recent past. Malkiel says that there do seem to be some time periods when a relative strength strategy would have outperformed a buy and hold strategy but that there is no evidence that it can do so consistently in the long-term. Likewise, "price volume" systems, which follow stocks that are rising on a large or increasing volume, are unlikely to produce good results.

So why is technical analysis so popular? Malkiel suggests that it is partly because it satisfies a human urge to do something, and partly because it encourages investors to trade frequently and is therefore promoted by commission-earning brokers.

While technical analysis is clearly unscientific, fundamental analysis is more plausible. It has three main flaws, however:

1. The company information used, and its analysis, may simply be wrong.
2. Estimates of intrinsic value may be wrong.
3. The stock price may not converge on the intrinsic value of the company for many years or ever.

It is not possible to predict the future accurately and consistently. Fundamental analysts are not really using "hard science," nor do they pretend to do so. To perform their often complex calculations they must make all kinds of assumptions about the companies they examine. The valuations they produce are based on forecasts of future earnings – a slight alteration to an estimate of future earnings greatly changes the price/earnings ratio that the estimate implies, and yet the estimates cannot, by their nature, be precise. Professionals, *en masse*, do not outperform the market averages and there are plenty of studies to show that analysts are not very good at estimating the future earnings of companies in the short-, medium- or long-term. Talented or lucky individuals may have good track records as analysts, but one cannot codify the fundamental approach and turn it into a real science.

So what's the answer? Malkiel discusses the mathematics of risk at some length. He tells us that one of the few things that we can be sure of is that risk and reward are correlated. If you take more risks, either by choosing riskier companies, or by adopting a riskier investment method, then your chances of making a large profit or suffering a large loss are increased. The problem is how to measure this. He describes various attempts, such as "beta" and "modern portfolio theory," but shows that they are, at best, inadequate.

Many academics have come to the conclusion that the "random walk" theory is the most satisfactory explanation of the market. The random walk, or "efficient market," theory has, according to Malkiel, three main versions, but in essence the idea is that the way that information is received by professional investors – who make up, in dollar terms, most of the market, is so efficient that any genuine bargains or price anomalies are quickly bid up to their "market" price.

The market is so efficient at adjusting to this new information that all anyone can realistically hope for is to perform as well as the overall average market return which, in the long term, has proved to be the best investment in real (inflation-adjusted) terms, beating bonds, property, collectibles and bank deposits by a healthy margin. To perform in line with the market averages used to be difficult but is now easier because of the availability of index tracker funds which hold the same stocks, in the same proportion, as the index which they follow. All you do is load up on the fund and forget about it.

Frustrated by this answer? Malkiel seems to be too. The three versions of the random walk are:

1. *The strong* – "absolutely nothing that is known or even knowable about a company will benefit the fundamental analyst."

2. *The semi-strong* – "no published information will help the analyst to select under-valued securities."

3. *The weak* – "past movements of stock prices are no guide to future movements."

He emphasises that that the idea of the random walk is *not* that stock prices are random or are insensitive to fundamental information but that they respond too rapidly to the information to allow individuals to obtain bargains.

Malkiel says that he, personally, is "not as ready as many of my academic colleagues to damn the entire field" (of professional advisers). He suggests that private investors might be well advised to put their money into funds run by outstanding managers such as John Neff, John Templeton and Dean LeBaron. He thinks that direct investment in individual equities is "too much fun to give up." He doubts that there really is perfect pricing in the market or that all information about stocks moves instantaneously. He repeats a joke about the finance professor who is walking with his student in the street and comes upon a $10 bill. The professor tells his student that the $10 is not really there because someone would have picked it up already. The student picks up the money anyway.

The book ends with a large and useful section of general advice to the investor. It is mostly the standard material that is widely available – that there is a life cycle to investing, the importance of regular saving, the effectiveness of dollar/cost averaging, the power of compound interest and so on, but it is helpful to have it set in the context of the "random walk." Malkiel outlines a number of strategies which you can adopt, depending on your circumstances; the main one is to buy appropriate mutual funds and hold them for the very long-term, but he does offer some advice for people who want to invest in individual equities.

This book is the clearest exposition of the opposing theories about the stock market that I've ever seen. While you may decide that the efficient market theory is unsatisfactory, you still need to understand it – it's a powerful antidote to the unrealistic expectations created by the legions of investment people who want you to hand over your money to them.

REMINISCENCES OF A STOCK OPERATOR

by

Edwin Lefèvre

"D'yeh see them?" he asked. "See what?" "Them guys.
Take a look at them kid. There's three hundred of 'em!
Three hundred suckers! Then yeh come in, and in two
days yeh cop more than I get out of the three hundred in
two weeks. That ain't business, kid – not for me! I ain't got
nothin' agin yeh. Yer welcome to what ye've got. But yeh
don't get any more. There ain't any here for yeh!"

(Lefèvre, page 28)

Material quoted within this chapter is extracted from *Reminiscences of a Stock
Operator* by Edwin Lefèvre, Books of Wall Street, Fraser Management
Associates, Burlington, 1980.

Back in the olden days at the beginning of the century, when the USA was not a superpower and its economic growth rates were like those of today's emerging markets, the trading of company stocks was not as orderly and controlled as it is now. *Reminiscences of a Stock Operator*, first published in 1923, is a collection of one speculator's memoirs, as told to the journalist Edwin Lefèvre. The speculator was, we are asked to believe, one Larry Livingston, but since the book is dedicated to the famous trader Jesse Laurston Livermore, this seems to be a mild fiction intended to protect Livermore and the author from lawsuits.

It's a great story, and Lefèvre tells it well. We enter a world glamorized in the movies as an age when the Wild West was nearly dead but the brave new world of finance was only just beginning to dominate our lives. It would make a good movie. Whether or not we can learn investment lessons from the book is another matter.

One lesson we always learn from reading old books about the markets is that people never seem to change – as Livingston/Livermore points out. All the cunning and folly and mixed motives of human nature were there then and are still with us today. But this is no organized, defined exposition of an experienced professional's view of the markets – it's a collection of tales told by a risk-addict, someone who made and lost millions several times over and claims to have enjoyed the process.

Livingston starts out at 14 as a quotation-board boy, posting stock price changes in a brokerage for the benefit of the customers. He begins to record the price fluctuations of active stocks and becomes fascinated by the patterns he sees. He feels that he can often predict when a stock is about to move sharply. This private mind game keeps him happy until one day another boy asks him to come in with him on a play on a company called Burlington. Livingston is astonished; to him, only the customers, rich old men, have enough money to actually operate in the market. The boy introduces him to bucket shops, operations which allowed people to gamble in a small way on stock price movements; they had the appearance of being brokers, but were actually betting shops, keeping a book for their customers rather than actually purchasing stock on their behalf.

Livingston's notebook tells him that Burlington should be going up, so he and his friend put up a total of $5 at the bucket shop. They win, and Livingston is hooked. Soon he is making enough money to leave his job and start gambling full time. By the time he is 15, he's made $1000. Soon he has to move from bucket shop to bucket shop as they tire of his success and begin to turn him away. The bucket shops, he says, in general played an honest game, but relied on the small margins and lack of resources of their customers to wipe them out on small fluctuations. As a customer, you weren't supposed to win consistently.

Finally there is only one bucket shop, a large chain, which will take his business, but only on disadvantageous terms. Despite this Livingston continues to be successful, so they try another tack. One day he has a short position of 3500 shares of sugar. As he watches the tape, he begins to sense that something is wrong with the way the sugar is behaving. Suddenly he closes his trades, to the great reluctance of the clerk – he has to raise his voice to insist that the transaction is completed (knowing that the bucket shops never wanted to get a reputation for reneging).

A few moments later the price of sugar begins to rise – if Livingston had held on he would have been wiped out. Evidently his short position, combined with that of another client, was enough to make it worth the bucket shop's while to get a broker in the real stock market to drive up the price of sugar for long enough to kill them. In those days, he tells us, it was not too hard to move the price of a semi-active stock if you knew what you were doing.

This narrow escape makes Livingston decide to go to New York and try his hand at trading on the real exchanges. Within six months he is wiped out. At the bucket shops he bought at the price shown on the tape and could sell instantaneously, but the real market isn't like that – he can't scalp in the same way because of the time lag between the prices on the floor and the prices shown on the ticker and also because it takes time for brokers to execute his orders. In effect, at the bucket shop he had been able to trade as if he had a seat on the exchange; now he is just another player, one step removed from the market, and in need of finding a new game with a longer time frame.

The picaresque tales roll on over the years; he makes and loses fortunes; he gets famous; he is blamed for sharp movements which are nothing to do with him. At one point he is so much in debt that he decides to go bankrupt. All his large creditors agree to renounce their claims on him. Soon he makes it all back and repays them in full. At another time he is wiped out and goes to Chicago where he finds a stake with which he trades in a small way. He is invited back to New York by the senior partner of a important brokerage, Williamson & Brown. Their largest client is a railroad man, Alvin Marquand, who is worth a fortune and also happens to be Williamson's brother-in-law.

Williamson invites Livingston to trade through his firm and hands him a check for $25 000. He explains that our hero's reputation as a big plunger will protect the operations of his "large clients" (which Livingston correctly divines refers exclusively to Marquand). Livingston agrees to the deal, starts trading and is soon in a position to pay the money back – but Williamson won't hear of it. Soon he begins to interfere with Livingston's trades, and to buy and sell in his name. Livingston realizes that he is being used. Marquand has died and Williamson is controlling him in order to sell Marquand's shares at the best prices – all to protect his sister, Marquand's widow. Livingston bears no grudges; his main frustration is that he has not been able to take advantage of ideal market conditions.

This book doesn't really tell you how to be trader but it does tell you what it is like to be one. Lefèvre has clearly labored long and hard to turn difficult material into a compelling story; we cannot know whether it depicts Livermore's life accurately, but it has an authentic flavor. What he doesn't tell us, but we now know, is that Livermore lost a fortune in the 1929 crash and never again achieved his previous success; in 1940 he shot himself.

Traders have peculiar personalities – if you meet a few, you soon learn to recognize the type. They often have excellent memories for numerical patterns; rarely do they have much patience or organizational ability. Like gamblers, they are often unhappy and are essentially uninterested in spending the money they earn – playing the game is far more important.

As portrayed in the book, Livingston/Livermore is not a sad case, but a man of his times. We are told very little about what else happens in his life, mainly, one suspects, because not much else did happen. Other more recent books by traders tell a similar tale; if Livermore were alive today, he'd be playing commodities and financial futures and, no doubt, loving every minute of it.

SOROS ON SOROS
STAYING AHEAD OF THE CURVE

by
George Soros
with
Byron Wien and
Krisztina Koenen

Classical economic theory assumes that market participants act on the basis of perfect knowledge. That assumption is false. The participants' perceptions influence the
market in which they participate, but the market action
also influences the participants' perceptions. They cannot
obtain perfect knowledge of the market because their
thinking is always affecting the market and the market is
affecting their thinking. This makes analysis of market
behavior much harder than it would be if the assumption
of perfect knowledge were valid.

(Soros, page 67)

Material quoted within this chapter is extracted from *Soros on Soros: Staying
Ahead of the Curve* by George Soros with Byron Wien and Krisztina Koenen,
John Wiley & Sons, Inc., New York, 1995.

There is something of a James Bond villain in George Soros. The billions, the old world charm, the heavyweight intellectuality combines with his audacious bets – there can be no other word for it – on the complex interplay of political and financial forces. As he says of himself:

> "If there was ever a man who would fit the stereotype of the Judaeo-plutocratic Bolshevik Zionist world conspirator, it is me. And that is, in fact, how I am increasingly depicted in Eastern Europe and also to some extent in Western Europe, but not so much in America. This is a prime example of how good deeds don't go unpunished."
>
> *(page 239)*

It is ironic that a Hungarian emigré, a survivor of wartime Europe, should be popularly perceived as sinister. When his offshore fund, the Quantum Fund, made $1 billion betting in 1992 that sterling would fall out of the ERM, the European Union's currency pegging system, he finally emerged into the public glare as that most awesome of urban myths, the international speculator. Every half-witted populist journalist and TV commentator piled in to build up a new demon in the mind of the public.

George Soros has a theory. It's called the "theory of reflexivity" which he delineates in his bizarre and opaque book *The Alchemy of Finance*, describing a 15-month "real time experiment" during which he increased the value of his fund from $647 million to $1.7 billion by a complex series of currency speculations, short selling, use of other derivatives and bond and commodity trading. As he himself tacitly admits, almost no-one understands his book. For this reason I have chosen *Soros on Soros* to represent this great modern trader because it delivers his ideas in a more accessible form.

Based on in-depth interviews in German with *Frankfurter Allegemeine Zeitung*, the book has been edited and amended by Soros himself. He tells us in the preface that he hopes the book will reach a wider audience than just those who are interested in the financial markets. This is because of his commitment to promoting "open society" across the world. What's an open society? Here's what he says:

> "In my philosophy, open society is based on the recognition that we all act on the basis of imperfect understanding. Nobody is in possession of the ultimate truth. Therefore, we need a critical mode of thinking; we need institutions and interests to live together in peace; we need a democratic form of government that ensures the orderly transfer of power; we need a market economy that provides feedback and allows mistakes to be corrected; we need to protect minorities and respect minority opnions. Above all, we need the rule of law ... An open society is one in which a person like me can live and prosper. As a Jew in Hungary I was hunted by the Nazis, then later I had a foretaste of communist rule in the country, so I know whereof I speak ...'

Part of the book deals with Soros's efforts to put these views into practice by means of substantial philanthropic donations he channels through several foundations, mainly in the ex-Soviet bloc and China.

Like many self-made men, Soros holds strong views on just about everything. Unusually, though, his views are actually interesting. His international perspective is the source of inspiration upon which he draws both to make his money and also try to change the world.

How did he get so rich? In 1953 he got a job as a trainee at the British brokers Singer & Friedlander, learning arbitrage. He was not successful, and in 1956 he applied for a visa for the US to take up a job at a New York brokerage. The visa only came through after Soros obtained an affidavit saying that arbitrage traders had to be young because they died young – at which point he resolved to get out of the business when he could!

Within a few years, he had become a successful analyst, specializing in European stocks which were then little understood in the US. Then President Kennedy introduced a 15 percent tax on foreign investments and business began to dry up. For three years Soros became preoccupied with writing philosophy, although he still held down his job, but in 1966 he decided to get back into the markets seriously.

This time he concentrated on picking US stocks, with some success, and started two funds for his employers. The second fund, the Double Eagle Fund, began in 1969 with $4 million; it was a "hedge" fund, allowed to sell stocks short and to borrow money. Leaving his employers on amicable terms, Soros set up the Soros Fund in 1973 with some of the stockholders of Double Eagle. It had capital of $12 million.

Soros took on a junior partner, Jim Rogers, now a famous investor in his own right. "Generally," says Soros, "we followed the principle of investing first and investigating. I did the investing and he did the investigating." They received 20 percent of the fund's profits, which they reinvested in its stock.

As the fund grew, (now renamed the Quantum Fund) the pair realized that they needed more staff but had difficulty in making the transition. Jim Rogers left. By 1979 Soros was worth, he estimates, about $25 million and the fund was worth $100 million. He had something of a psychological crisis, connected with recognizing his success, and for the next two years, having lost Rogers and his first wife, he ran the fund with much looser constraints. The fund did extremely well during this "rather wild period" – in two years it jumped from $100 million to $400 million.

Then he started to lose money. In 1981 the fund was down for the first time, by a whopping 22 percent. Investors started pulling out, and the fund shrank from $400 million to $200 million. Soros decided to turn Quantum into a fund of funds, farming out pieces of it to other managers and employing others to invest the rest.

This strategy did not produce very good returns. In 1984 Soros decided to write his book *The Alchemy of Finance* to restimulate his interest in investment, and, as part of the book, to take over active management of Quantum again as a "real-time experiment." This was, he says, an "alchemical" experiment, not a scientific one.

The experiment was based on Soros's hypothesis that the 1985 Plaza Accord, when the G5 nations decided to act together to depreciate the dollar, meant that the era of floating exchange rates was over – to be replaced by "dirty floating" (currency pegging). Soros bet heavily against the dollar by going long on the yen and the mark, shorting oil and going long on companies that were takeover candidates. For three weeks, the mark and the yen dropped, and Soros was losing heavily. Then the Plaza Accord was held, and the next day these currencies started to rise against the dollar. Soros massively increased his positions by borrowing. By November 1985 the fund had an exposure of about $4 billion, though its capital was only $800 million, in a complicated series of positions, short and long, in different markets. Rapidly adjusting his positions week by week, Soros won handsomely. The Quantum Fund appreciated by 114 percent during the 15 months of his "experiment."

In 1987 Soros made a bad move shorting Japan and lost heavily. He still made a 14 percent profit for the year, however. By this time he had acquired a management team, headed by Stanley Druckenmiller, and he started to concentrate on other things, notably his work in Eastern Europe, where revolution was in the air.

Over the 26 years from 1969 to 1995, the Quantum Fund made a 35 percent annual return overall, despite some wild losses.

These days, Soros leaves the work to his managers, retaining a "strategic role."

Until 1992, few people outside the industry had heard of him. Then came the UK's "Black Wednesday" when sterling fell out of the ERM. Soros talks in detail about why he thinks the ERM was flawed. He believes that the planned common European currency (EMU) is the death knell of the Bundesbank, which will be superseded by a European Central Bank. In his view, Germany after reunification required a different monetary policy from the rest of Europe and the pressures on the ERM were building.

When the head of the Bundesbank said in a speech that investors were wrong to think of the ECU as a fixed basket of currencies, Quantum "took the hint" and went short on the Italian lira which subsequently fell out of the ERM.

The next currency in danger was obviously sterling. Quantum's Druckenmiller wanted to short sterling and Soros agreed, advising him to "go for the jugular," leveraging more than normal. "We only had our equity at risk," he says, "In that kind of situation we could have risked our equity several times over."

Britain raised interest rates by 2 percent to defend sterling in the currency markets and Soros admits that Quantum might have pushed it over the edge at the very end because they continued to short sterling when other market players might have hesitated – but he believes that sterling would have gone anyway.

All of a sudden Soros was famous. He has stayed in the limelight ever since – Malaysia's premier loudly denounced him for his role – real or imagined – in the Asian currency crisis of 1997. People don't understand Soros's philosophy, his politics, his philanthropy, his trading methods or his fund, so it is hardly surprising that he is demonized. You don't get to be popular by appearing to be extremely smart – you have to dumb down to be liked, the way Buffett does. *Soros on Soros* is an attempt to redress the balance by explaining what he is all about. It succeeds to a limited extent, but I fear that Soros is doomed to remain a misunderstood philosopher/billionaire – the Lex Luthor of our age.

There is a Soros Foundation website at:

http://www.soros.org

TECHNICAL ANALYSIS
OF STOCK TRENDS

by
Robert D. Edwards
and John Magee

Stock prices move in trends. Some of those trends are straight, some are curved; some are brief and some are long-continued; some are irregular or poorly defined and others are amazingly regular or "normal," produced in a series of action and reaction waves of great uniformity. Sooner or later, these trends change direction; they may reverse (as from up to down) or they may be interrupted by some sort of sideways movement and then, after a time, proceed again in their former direction.

(Edwards and Magee, page 60)

Material quoted within this chapter is extracted from *Technical Analysis of Stock Trends* by Robert D. Edwards and John Magee, 7th edition, John Magee, Inc., Chicago, 1997.

Chartist friends assure me that this is the standard work on technical analysis, the art of reading charts. "It's a solid work," they assure me. "Nothing much that is original, but a good reference work." It certainly looks like a textbook, all 721 pages of it, packed with charts and diagrams. It looks heavyweight, the way that Graham and Dodd's *Security Analysis* looks on your bookshelves – reassuringly substantial.

As I read it, though, I am less reassured. It is vaguely reminiscent of those medieval books of sorcery, also substantial and expensive, which were packed with diagrams intended to give the practitioners power over the course of events. I begin to feel like a man from Mars – what can these strange earthlings be thinking? Are they serious about all this?

Greenhorn investors, the book tells me, tend to dismiss technical analysis, but no truly experienced player will do so. This is not true, but it is in any case beside the point, since the opinions of investors differ on many matters and that's how the market works – buyers and sellers have different opinions. Yet I think I know what the authors mean; technical analysis explores a territory that is familiar to all of us yet is very hard to measure, namely, what is everyone else going to do next? It aims to profit in the main from short-term movements. John Train has described charts of stock averages as the "encephalogram of the human race," meaning that the ways that prices move are a reflection of a great mass of human activity and volition – the behavior of consumers, employees and managers in the listed companies, and the behavior of investors, institutions and the professionals who help to supply the capital these businesses need.

In aggregate, the world's markets constitute a large portion of the whole of productive activity on the planet, and it shows. Markets do seem to react to wars, elections and other major events, and they do appear to react to what people in general are afraid of, or hopeful for, as well. Market players are not robots – they behave in human ways, so it seems legitimate to talk of market psychology. Technical analysis claims that this psychology can be "read" from the charts – all the formations, the flags, wedges, diamonds, double tops, right-angle triangles and so on, all lovingly illustrated and discussed in this book, are supposed to help you predict where the price will go next. Somehow the mass mind behaves repetitively. It's an attractive idea, and sociologists make a lot of hay out of it, yet so far there has been no really adequate body of knowledge to give us a real handle on it. How the chartists identified these patterns is not really clear – by experience, they say – but if they really exist, perhaps one could apply them to other matters – predicting politics, for instance, or the course of wars.

Elsewhere in the book other ways of approaching these mysteries are discussed in detail – randomness, probability, market efficiency and so on. None of these is entirely satisfactory; as pointed out in *Against the Gods* (*see* pages 1–10), the results of taking statistical samples do not give you absolute certainty, only a degree of likelihood. This is the human condition; we can not be absolutely certain of anything at all. Take medicine – not all diseases can be cured, irrespective of the money you spend or the brilliance of the specialists involved.

Despite this uncertainty, we have to live on, using assumptions and estimates, or retire from the world. Bertrand Russell said of the philosopher Wittgenstein (I'm paraphrasing) that "He wouldn't admit that there was not a rhinoceros in the room," that is, that he was ever conscious of our inability to be certain. This is one of the great existential riddles, and I have every sympathy with the majority of people, who feel uncomfortable at this thought and prefer to find refuge in the arms of any number of ideologies and belief systems.

In any case, we who like making money are certain that we want it. I think. And perhaps you can find some common ground with chartism. Most of us speak in terms of bull and bear markets, for example. So does Dow Theory. Most of us would like to get out before a bull market busts and get in just after the end of a bear market. Or, if we're short sellers, the other way around. At the time of writing, we seem to be in one of the longest bull markets ever – if you regard the 1987 crash as a "correction," then it's been going for some two decades. All the actuaries I know have been saying for years that the markets are overvalued. Prices are still going up. They must go down some time (I don't know how I can be so sure, but I am); if that happens in a hurry, maybe I'll take a big loss because I'm not watching. Maybe I should put in my stop-loss order now. Maybe … I hesitate to say this, but maybe I should study the charts to see if there are any "technical" signs that the market is topping out. Just to see, you understand – I'm still a fundamentalist really. This is what the institutions do. They keep a few chartists on the staff – the overhead is not great – just for insurance.

Since I think that I cannot be certain about anything, I cannot be certain that technical analysis is completely useless. In *The Pitfalls of Speculation* (Moody's, 1906) Thomas Gibson wrote that the notion underlying chartism is "untrustworthy, absolutely fatuous and highly dangerous." Perhaps he is right.

Or, a happier thought, perhaps technical analysis is in some prescientific phase, and has empirically discovered real phenomena in market behavior. Perhaps in a century or so there will be a new science of pattern watching that really works, every time – the numbers of its practitioners would have to be limited, like the number of lawyers, or else everyone's collective efforts would cancel each other's out (i.e., the market would be efficient).

Then I wake from this reverie. This book cost me $75, and I'd rather have given the 75 bucks to a sympathetic lady fortune teller who would at least have tried to make me feel better. The book is important, the way that *Das Kapital* and *Mein Kampf* are important – they are important historical documents and you don't have to agree with what is in them to know that they are important. *Ça suffit*, as the French say. Please don't write me any letters about chartism – I'm certain that I won't reply.

THINK LIKE A TYCOON

by

W. G. Hill

... Don't be a consumer. If your mind is always focused on how to blow the next few hundred dollars, you'll never accumulate the capital you need to be successful.

(Hill, page 24)

Material quoted within this chapter is extracted from *Think Like a Tycoon* by W. G. Hill, 5th edition, Scope International Ltd, Waterlooville, 1993.

In the investment business most people have one personal favorite self-help book and this is mine. It's eccentric, hard-to-find, overpriced, full of hyperbole and errors of detail, but I love it just the same. The lessons it contains can serve you well in your pursuit of wealth.

In *The Money Game* (*see* pages 159–165), Adam Smith points out that if you want to get really, really rich, you shouldn't be an outside investor in the stock-market, you should go into business. *Think Like a Tycoon* tells you how. Many investors have unrealistic expectations of their stocks and are driven to take more and more risks. If you have the time and energy, you could do better by taking action. Instead of giving your money to others in the hope of a good return, as stock investors do, you can try to do it for yourself.

Being in business for yourself is not for everyone, and there are many small business people who never get rich. There are a number of reasons why this is the case, but one of the most important ones is that people go into the wrong business in the first place. It's often said that most tycoons make their money in finance, and real estate. *Think Like a Tycoon* is largely about investing in real estate.

Another barrier to personal wealth creation is a psychological one – many of us would like to go into business, but we haven't gathered the inner strength to do so. This is why self-help books are useful, even if they seem a little dumb sometimes. To gather your strength and take the first few steps, you need pep talks from a coach – and when you don't have a coach, the right book can do the job.

Bill Hill tells us that his principles can be applied to any business – and certainly the self-help part of *Think Like a Tycoon* can. He says that many people around us will try to convince us that either it can't be done, you can't get rich, or that making money is boring or immoral. "So ignore the socialist do-gooders," says Hill, "they don't produce products or services. All they want to do is make us feel guilty." He talks at length about the ways we thwart ourselves. Do you think you're too dumb? That's OK, lots of rich people are dumb, and all the smart people are in grad school instead getting out there and making money. No start-up capital? Doesn't matter. No experience? Get some.

Here's Hill's "Tycoon's Credo":

"A Tycoon is:

1. *Organized.* I will schedule a written program of my activities and objectives and stick to it the entire day.
2. *Dedicated.* I will do at least one thing I should have done, but have been putting off.
3. *Confident.* I will feel as good as possible and achieve a sense of well-being by meditating 15 minutes every day. I will exercise or jog another 15 minutes.
4. *Appreciative.* I will tell my family, friends and business associates "I like you" and mean it. I will be generous with praise and compliments.
5. *Optimistic.* I will not dwell on past failures but will think pos-

itively about the present and the future.

6. *Educated.* I will read something to improve my mind each day, and will keep away from non-productive and time-consuming people and activities.

7. *Thrifty.* I will not be a consumer or a taxpayer any more than is absolutely necessary.

8. *Sociable.* I will be charming and agreeable to everyone and speak badly of no one.

9. *Alert.* I will be open to new ideas, experiences, and people who might teach me something new, and I will not let myself fall into a rut or routine.

10. *Dependable.* I will meet all business, social, and moral obligations punctually, honestly, and honorably."

(pages 83 and 84)

This list may sound silly, or too obvious, but it works. Succeeding in business is not about complexity – it's about keeping things manageable. A real-life self-made tycoon I know (who is dyslexic), always says "Keep things simple." "Complicated" may get you a job as a wage slave, but "simple" makes you money in business.

Now for the hard part; how to make the money. Investing in real estate is an unusual business because it is relatively easy to get large amounts of credit in the form of loans secured on the properties you buy. Hill recommends leveraging to the hilt, servicing the debt from the rental income and waiting for inflation to bring you a capital gain.

It works like this:

- Borrow $100 000 to purchase a house with nothing, or almost nothing, down.
- Rent out the house and use the money to make the repayments and maintain the building.
- After some time sell the property. If you receive only the equivalent price to what you paid, inflation will have brought you a profit, e.g., if inflation totaled 15 percent over the period, you get a $15 000 profit after you pay back the mortgage.

It gets better – there are ways of buying low and adding value to properties which can bring you extra profits. There are ways of borrowing which give you plenty of liquidity (real estate itself is decidedly illiquid). There are ways of pyramiding yourself into a property empire very quickly. There are ways of borrowing so that you can walk away from the liability if the deal goes bad (in banking this is known as "moral hazard").

In the real estate game you get a lot of trouble with people. Watch out for the "Double eSSers," says Hill. These are the people who will screw and sue you, the people who want things they are not entitled to. His advice is to settle with them quickly and cut them out of your life – court cases are money-wasting, unproductive and emotionally draining.

The same goes for you too – "Don't you be a double eSSer," he says. And don't be a deadbeat. At the first sign of trouble – a cashflow problem, say – the deadbeat fails to cope. He goes away, or won't answer the phone. If you have a problem, face up to it and go and talk to your bankers; they hate foreclosing and would much rather give you a chance to resolve the problem.

This is really good advice. In my own life, I've watched business people fritter away inheritances because they couldn't face their problems. One man I know grew up in a mansion and inherited a business employing 30 people. Within three years he had spent all his cash and sent the business into bankruptcy. He know lives in two rooms over a grocery store. Why? He was one of nature's deadbeats, who couldn't face up to reality when anything went wrong, however minor. Business is one damn thing after another – so get used to it and face up to your obligations, or you'll go bust.

So how do you start in real estate? Go and look at hundreds of properties as a prospective purchaser and also pretending to be a tenant. Values and potential rental income will be exaggerated by sellers and agents, while the true expenses will be understated. By looking at a large number of properties you get a feel for the market in that area and a much better idea of real values.

Once you've looked at at least 100 properties, Hill says you should make a low offer on every single one. The point is that all properties are worth something, if only for the land they are on; if you buy at the right price you can make a profit on the most unpromising building.

Doesn't sound much like the stockmarket? Well we can certainly see some parallels – researching properties is like fundamental analysis, and buying low is what Warren Buffett does. The real difference though is that real estate is a highly *inefficient* market, whatever anyone tells you to the contrary. It is localized, neither the retail customers nor the agents have full knowledge of all the properties available, there are many legal anomalies, turnover is comparatively low and much value can be added by simple improvements. Naturally, many people will tell you that this is not so, but I know that Bill Hill is correct on this point. A knowledgeable operator can root out bargains and make above-average profits – the book mentions auctions, probates, conservatorships and foreclosures as having potential.

If you can make a profit on one building, you can do the same on hundreds of buildings. That's how you get to be a tycoon. To do that you need to build up your line of credit, and to do that you need to be in the game. A word of warning – many highly-leveraged real estate tycoons go broke during a general collapse in prices. This is the one issue that Hill does not tackle adequately. There are ways of protecting yourself against total disaster, even when you are very highly leveraged. Essentially you need to have a plan for the crisis – you need to know how to walk away from some deals, and you need to diversify across markets.

Before that happens, though, you have to get rich in the first place. To get rich you don't have to be clever, talented or good-looking – but you do have to really, really want to get rich! I enjoy this book; I hope you do too.

TRADER VIC
METHODS OF A
WALL STREET MASTER

by
Victor Sperandeo
with T. Sullivan Brown

My objective as a trader has always been to obtain and maintain the freedom secured by financial independence; consequently, my goal has been to make money consistently, month in and month out, year after year. I have always approached my career as a *business*, and a prudent businessman wants to first cover his overhead each month and then concentrate on achieving a steady growth in earnings. Rather than striving for the big hit, I protect capital first and work for consistent returns, and take more aggressive risk with a portion of the profits. Not accidentally, the big hits still come along: but they come along without excessive risk.

(Sperandeo, page 21)

Material quoted within this chapter is extracted from *Trader Vic: Methods of a Wall Street Master* by Victor Sperandeo with T. Sullivan Brown, John Wiley & Sons, Inc., New York, 1993.

This is one of the less useful books of the 25 classics. I decided to include it, however, partly because it is a bestseller and evidently has a constituency of fans, and also because if you want to know what goes on in the minds of successful traders you must listen to what they have to say. Two things are certain about Victor Sperandeo – he is a successful trader and he has a lot to say.

Sperandeo gives his trading results in some detail. For the decade 1978–87 he shows a nominal annual rate of return of 70.71 percent. His monthly gross profit/loss figures show admirably few loss-making months for the period 1972–1987, which appears to support his contention that one

> "should be able to capture between 60 and 80 percent of the long-
> term price trend (whether up or down) between bull market tops
> and bear market bottoms in any market … the focus should be on
> making consistent profits at low risk."

Like other traders, he stresses the importance of not risking all your capital at once. His advice to a beginner in commodities starting with, say, $50 000, is to take an initial position of not more than $5000 and set "exit points" to limit a possible loss to 10 percent to 20 percent (e.g., $500–$1000). If the first trade results in a loss of $1000, he suggests that you take your next position with only $4000, and so on. If you have a winning first trade of, say, $2000, he says that you should bank half of the profit and add the remainder to your $5000 for the next trade. If you have a series of winning trades you should increase the sum at risk proportionately each time. Each year, he tells us, he himself limited the amount of initial capital he was willing to risk: $250 000 during 1972–76, $500 000 in 1977, $2 million during 1978–86 and $100 000 in 1987. All the rest of the profits were banked for safety.

So far, so good. Sperandeo is a believer in the Dow Theory in its original form, as promulgated by Charles Dow, William Hamilton and Robert Rhea. He asserts that the theory still holds good for today's markets. He has performed a study applying the Dow Theory to the industrial and railroad averages (later the transportation averages) from 1896 to 1985 which showed its effectiveness, says Sperandeo, stating that, among other examples, Dow Theory would have had you short during the 1987 crash. This study is unpublished.

Sperandeo goes on to expound the Dow Theory at some length, reaffirming Robert Rhea's three "hypotheses."

1. That the primary trend cannot be manipulated, but the secondary trend and the day-to-day movement can be.
2. The closing prices of the Dow Jones rail and industrial averages, when charted, anticipate "coming events" and respond quickly to natural disasters.
3. The Dow Theory is not infallible.

Even to a non-technician, these three statements do not seem to be entirely objectionable. Sperandeo then goes on to discuss the five "theorems" of Dow Theory as set down by Rhea.

1. The averages have three trends, a primary that may last for sev-

eral years, a secondary that may last from three weeks to three months and a tertiary, which is the daily fluctuation. (The author adds that these trends may be moving in different directions from one another and that they apply to all markets.)

2. The primary trend is the bull or bear market and must be correctly identified. Its duration cannot be correctly predicted.

3. Primary bear markets are in three phases (connected with investor psychology): here Sperandeo gives a number of figures from his own research, such as the statement that 75 percent of all bear markets last between 0.8 and 2.8 years.

4. Primary bull markets are also in three phases. (The author adds more data, including the statement that 75 percent of all bull markets in history have lasted more than 1.8 years)

5. Secondary reactions are a reversal in the primary trend lasting three weeks to three months, during which the prices retrace between 33 percent and 66 percent of the price at the end of the previous secondary reaction.

Now that you have got the basics, says Sperandeo, it is time to study price trends more deeply. "If you know what the trend is, and if you know when it is most likely to change, then you really have all the knowledge you need to make money in the markets." He then plunges into more chartism.

Perhaps one day I will have a Pauline conversion to chartism, but these chapters have left me unconvinced. In fairness to the author, it is plain that he does apply these ideas in making his profitable trades – this is no starving chartist in a garret.

Sperandeo has strong views about program trading, which he describes as the attempt by institutions to manipulate markets by "playing the disparities in prices between related markets, disparities often induced or exaggerated by their own activities."

Program trading, he explains, exploits the way in which the independent traders behave in the markets. He gives an interesting example – a $2 billion pension fund wants to sell $100 million of its stocks. It knows that this sale will push indexes lower, so it picks a quiet period, "usually around 2 pm," to sell the S & P index short by $200 million. At about 3.10, the fund starts selling its stock in amounts of around $10 million every five minutes, ending with one big sale just before the market closes. This activity encourages other traders to sell short and prices move downwards, followed by the futures market. The fund makes large gains on its short futures contracts which amply compensate for any notional losses on its stock sales. The next day the markets go back up to where it was and the fund makes more profits by trading in a similar way.

Furthermore, he quotes the point of William O'Neil that the financial institutions are allowed to have direct computer links with the NYSE's computers and thus obtain instant execution for their orders, while the rest of us must wait a few minutes to have our orders executed.

The strongly expressed opinions continue on a wide range of topics, some of them interesting, others less so. Sperandeo is an admirer of the writer Ayn Rand and dislikes Keynes (*see* pages 133–140), principally it seems because he dislikes centralized government. He writes at length in a rather undisciplined way about economics in general and what is wrong with America in particular. In short, he is like many successful businessmen who chafe at the regulatory ties that bind us all.

He is for more freedom. The last section of the book is virtually a self-help text, admonishing us not to think money is everything, to enjoy our lives, not to get carried away by our pride and so on. A lot of it makes sense and is plainly sincerely felt, but all in all, this book contains a great deal of opinion, oversimplification and "off-topic" material which some readers may find useful, but many will find redundant.

Many successful traders are not literary types. It's quite unusual for them to write books about their work, so *Trader Vic* is a rarity and, as an authentic expression of a trader's thoughts, a classic.

WHERE ARE THE CUSTOMERS' YACHTS?

OR A GOOD HARD LOOK AT WALL STREET

by

Fred Schwed Jr

Investment and speculation are said to be two different things, and the prudent man is advised to engage in the one and avoid the other. This is something like explaining to the troubled adolescent that love and passion are two different things. He perceives that they are different but they don't seem quite different enough to clear up his problems.

(Schwed, Jr, page 171)

Material quoted within this chapter is extracted from *Where are the Customers' Yachts: Or a Good Hard Look at Wall Street* by Fred Schwed Jr, John Wiley & Sons, Inc., New York, 1995.

There's no doubt that the investment world is ridiculous, but it's rare to find a truly funny investment book. This is one.

The title of the book comes from an old joke – the story being that a visitor from out of town was being shown around New York's financial district. When they got to the Battery, the guide pointed out the bankers' and brokers' yachts, at which the visitor asked, "Where are the customers' yachts?"

Fred Schwed spent a few years on Wall Street in the 1920s. Michael Lewis (author of *Liar's Poker, see* pages 141–148) tells us in his introduction that Schwed had been expelled from Princeton in his senior year for having a girl in his room in the evening and that he preferred golf and drinking to work. The tone of *Where are the Customers' Yachts?* is one of wry observation and gentle tolerance – what you might describe as "P. G. Wodehouse meets the *New Yorker*" – of a very crazy world.

An easy read, yes, but also a good hard look at the why, not just the how, of Wall Street. Schwed talks sense. Something of an efficient marketeer long before the concoction of the theory, his main theme is the difficulty of being able to guess what a stock price is going to do next. He finds professional approaches no less futile than the amateur's; here, for example, is a story he tells about a statistician, as analysts were then called:

"When a statistician works up a sufficient reputation for profundity, he is graduated and becomes an economist. There was an economist who never went anywhere without his many briefcases, which were the fattest and heaviest known to the fiscal world. He was in big demand and attended conferences all over, but he was not the athletic type, so office boys had to lug the brief cases. I once found myself in an elevator with one of these boys. He was sagging under the briefcases and looked like a melancholy dray horse.

'Those belong to Mr. Z?' I asked.

'Uh-huh,' he replied, with no enthusiasm.

'Listen,' I said, 'Here is an idea. Why don't you kids paste a little strip of paper inside the zippers? Then you could find out whether he ever opens those brief cases.'

'We did,' said the moody office boy. 'He don't.'"

(page 40)

While frequently puncturing the aura of omnipotence surrounding market professionals, Schwed makes no personal claim to superior investment ability. In fact, he constantly points out his own inability to get it right. He buys, holds and sells, and then a long time later realizes that he should have kept on holding. In the first edition he makes some slightly disparaging remarks about investment trusts, and, in his introduction written some 15 years later, tells us that he sold his shares in one after they had doubled, intending to repurchase them when they fell to a more realistic level. They never did.

To a neophyte this may seem unhelpful; someone, after all, must be making profits. Most of us do, in fact, in bull markets – and, overall, in the long term, actuaries tell us we all can expect an annual real rate of return of about 3 percent, a deeply unexciting figure which perhaps explains why people are so eager to find ways of doing better.

To do better, you have to take on more risk, and one of the riskiest forms of investment is derivatives. For most of the century derivatives have been rather less exotic beasts than they are now, but Schwed's remark that "the subject, like pinochle, is not profound but it is complex" still holds true. Today's derivative fiends – mainly young traders working for financial institutions – assure us that the principal *raison d'être* of derivatives is as a hedge against potential risk in other holdings, but catastrophic losses, such as the ones which brought down the dignified old British merchant bank, Barings, suggest otherwise. The basic problem is well defined here: "is the price of the insurance [i.e., the hedge] commensurate with the amount of the protection obtained?" He goes on to say, talking of options, that the answer cannot be solved mathematically, a statement with which many of today's derivatives traders might not agree.

It's a truism to say that investment psychology never changes, despite the extraordinary growth of the world's economy, and the apparent sophistication of investment techniques. Human nature doesn't change, and a little understanding of people can take you a long way in the markets. The average private investor cannot afford to spend every waking moment studying the market, hence the argument for hiring a pro to do the job. Assuming that you find an adviser who is honest you can invest with reasonable safety; unfortunately, says the author, he does not know exactly what "reasonable safety" means.

While he allows the possibility that "the greatest of investment mistakes is trying for too high a return with its attendant tragic risk," he goes on to describe those professional advisers who play it so safe as to deliver almost no real return at all, justifying their fees by the security of their clients' capital and the fact that they themselves have not stolen any of it.

It is one of the ironies of investment that people who want total security end up almost guaranteeing themselves a loss. Consider this problem from the point of view of investment advisers: if you were a pro who had clients who looked as if they might sue you if their portfolios went down a few points, what are you going to put them into? Bonds, most likely, which, even if index-linked, are not likely to provide a good return.

Fred Schwed is no great fan of the Securities and Exchange Commission (SEC) either. He feels that the reputed crookedness of the markets – which the SEC was founded to police – is overestimated. He believes that the regulatory legislation of his day has done little or nothing to prevent market volatility, which was then popularly perceived to be the result of price manipulation. Today the public is more sophisticated; volatility has not been abolished and we have new theories to explain it that do not rely on the demonization of the professionals. Yet with the recent currency crisis in Asia, as in most previous crises across the world, politicians have been eager to tell their constituents that the problems have been caused by those devils incarnate, the professional speculators (a.k.a. George Soros and others). *Plus ça change* ... Regulation is political because it is controlled by politicians and is thus subject to the violent moods of the populace who, naïvely but understandably, hate to lose money.

Schwed tells an entertaining story of a broker who, in 1937, was suspended for 90 days for buying National Kelvinator at $5 on the day of a sudden drop (the share's price had been $11 on the previous day); the following day the price was back at $11 and the broker made a tidy profit. Schwed points out that a man who had made such a profit might be happy to take a holiday with his family for three months during the suspension period and thus that the punishment was hardly effective. He asks what crime had actually been committed and whether the SEC would have been willing to bid anything at all for National Kelvinator at the time of the price drop. The fact that the broker had held on to the shares for an aeon of 23 minutes when the price began to rise again is hardly excessive and in any case would he have been punished for losing money if the price had not bounced back?

Regulatory authorities admittedly have a difficult job. Insider dealing is very, very hard to prove and the first place to look for it is amongst those happy few who have suddenly made large profits. The making of profits is not in itself a crime, and indeed Schwed confesses to a "sneaking fondness for that wretched old hag, the capitalist system, after watching the performance of her temperamental younger rivals."

In fact, I sense that Schwed came up against the horrors of greed early in life; he's a philosopher, gently reminding us not to get too excited about our attempts to make a quick buck and pointing out that "real" things, like homes, families and good times are more important than paper profits or investment "head trips." He does this with charm and style.

The cartoons in the book illustrate the author's philosophy well; my favorites are the image of a middle-aged man sounding off to his wide-eyed spouse, captioned, "The average male likes to sit at breakfast and tell his wife and children what Adolf Hitler is going to do month after next" and a picture of a younger man in evening dress singing and playing the piano in close proximity to two voluptuous and slightly drunk ladies, captioned, "How would it have been if he had just stayed at home with his $300 000?"

The book certainly makes for light reading, but this masks its true profundity. Its simple language and delightful style could easily lead the casual reader to assume that it is superficial, making cheap shots at easy targets. Yet the fact that a book is enjoyable to read does not necessarily mean that it is insubstantial, and *Where Are the Customers' Yachts?* manages to delineate the very real paradoxes that lie at the center of the business of investment. We can't predict the future. Our multiplicity of instincts drive us to do foolish things with capital. People who can't master probability and risk should stay away from direct investment. Don't watch your investments and forget to watch your own state of mind – do you really need to send your daughter to an expensive finishing school, for instance? He covers most of the bases and, in my view, he's right.

The book offers real market wisdom for those who invest to live rather than live to invest.

INDEX